ROBOTZ

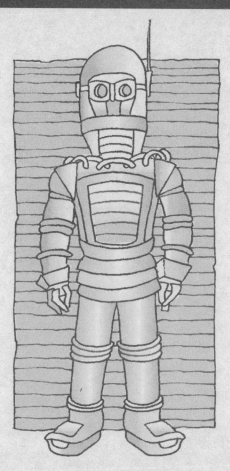

ROBOTZ

An Encyclopedia of Robots in Fact and Fiction

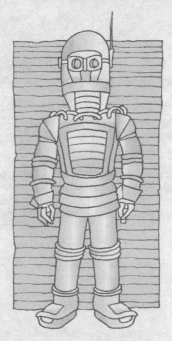

Stephen Munzer

SCHOLASTIC INC.

New York   Toronto   London   Auckland   Sydney
Mexico City   New Delhi   Hong Kong   Buenos Aires

To my parents
Dennis and Betty

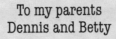

ISBN 0-439-43118-2

Text © 2002 by Stephen Munzer.
Illustrations © 2002 by Stephen Munzer.

All rights reserved. Published by Scholastic Inc., 557 Broadway, New York,
NY 10012, by arrangement with The Chicken House.

SCHOLASTIC and associated logos are trademarks and/or registered
trademarks of Scholastic Inc. THE CHICKEN HOUSE and associated
logos are trademarks of The Chicken House.

12 11 10 9 8 7 6 5 4 3 2 1   2 3 4 5 6 7/0

Printed in the U.S.A.
First Scholastic printing, September 2002

CONTENTS

Introduction

How would you like a robot of your very own? Imagine what cool fun you could have. The next time your mom gives you a dirty look and tells you to clean up your room, you could set your obedient robot to work on the task, clearing away that pile of smelly socks and mountain of empty potato chip bags.

CYBER-SERVANT

It doesn't take long to think of all the wonderful things a Robo-pal could do. How about taking the dog for a walk when you're tired out? What about washing dishes, doing your math home-work, mowing the lawn, cleaning the car, straightening out the neighborhood bully ... the possibilities are endless. Let's face it — with a cyber-servant you need never work again!

THE CHOICE IS YOURS

Have you ever thought about what your ideal robot would be like? Would you choose the "Robby, the Robot" style, with awesome metal arms and a goldfish bowl for a head? Or would you prefer the human-style android with a friendly smile and natural skin effect? Perhaps you'd go for a cute little robot like R2-D2 with wheels instead of legs. The choices are endless.

ROBOT PAST

Of course, you wouldn't be the first to dream of having an artificial life-form to help out with all the ordinary tasks you have to do each day. People have been imagining and trying to build robotlike helpers for thousands of years. The ancient Greeks had them; so did the Chinese and Egyptians. In the Middle Ages and over the past few hundred years, inventors have worked with cogs and gears, pulleys and weights, to build clockwork human and animal figures that walk, talk, write, and play musical instruments. They named them "automata" or "androids."

ROBOT PRESENT

Modern scientists have electricity, computers, and all sorts of techno-toys to play with, so they really can work miracles and build robots with lives of their very own.

Stories, books, and films have shown fabulous fictitious robots to excite our imaginations and entertain us. They give a tantalizing taste of what might be in store for us in the future.

If you've ever been to a big theme park like Disneyland, you've probably seen animatronic robots like pirates, ghosts, cowboys, and famous historical heroes in action. Some are very realistic indeed. Other robots don't look like people at all. They may have clever mechanical arms that can build cars, or genius brains that can play chess against human grand masters. Look around and you'll be amazed how many robots are already at work among us.

ROBOT FUTURE

In your lifetime there will be many more. Who knows? When you're old, there may be robot shop assistants to help with all those grocery bags, android teachers in the classroom, and even a robot butler in your home. It's very likely, however, that most robots will be so small that you won't see them at all. Tiny "nano-bots," no bigger than a speck of dust may be swimming around in your bloodstream, repairing damage to your body and keeping you alive until you're over two hundred years old. They may be hidden in homes and offices everywhere, quietly doing a thousand jobs to make life easier for us all.

YOUR PERSONAL GUIDE

In this A–Z Guide you'll find lots of amazing robots. You'll discover robots in fiction and get the lowdown on robot technology today. There are robots to entertain, teach, sing, dance, and DJ! Some can be found at the bottom of the sea and some far out in space, heading for the edge of the solar system on a journey to the stars.

Your future awaits you!

A NOTE ABOUT THE SYMBOLS

Throughout this book you will see the following symbols. They help to classify each robot in one of four ways.

 These are robots that have been built in real life to do a particular job. They operate all by themselves or through computer programming. Some are very old and some are at the cutting edge of today's technology. Whether ancient or modern, these guys mean business and that's a fact!

 These robots are made to be played with. They are more than mere objects to be gazed at and admired. These bots don't mind a little "rough and tumble." So let's test them to the limit and see what they're made of!

 People have been writing about robot creations ever since the first wise guy invented the alphabet. Through the ages, brilliant storytellers using just the power of words have sparked the imagination with tales of mechanical people. If your favorite robot turns out to be a fictitious flight of fancy, then you'll find it here.

 These include robots on TV as well as movie stars. Most are played by human actors in robot costumes, or operated as fancy puppets with strings and wires to make them appear real. Some of the most modern cyber-stars are created in the world of virtual reality with powerful computer programs. And don't forget the "techno-toons" — those robot cartoon characters created with little more than a 2B pencil and a paintbrush.

Aaron

If you think that robots are only fit for lifting heavy steel girders or working out mega-tricky math problems in less than a nanosecond, then hold it right there! Just like humans, some of them can be creative and paint pretty pictures of daisies, bunnies, and sailing boats.

CREATOR

After 23 years of research, Professor Harold Cohen, a painter himself, built Aaron — the world's first robot artist. It cost him $150,000 to develop, although Aaron's paintings can easily sell for $2,000 apiece. So what do you think . . . how many pictures does he need to paint to repay the professor for all his hard work?

HOW DOES IT WORK?

During the night Aaron designs five or six paintings in his central processor and stores them safely in his memory. The following day he sets about painting one of his designs. This can take five or six hours. Aaron mixes up his own colors and even cleans his brushes and paint palette afterward — not bad for a machine with less intelligence than the average earthworm.

AF 709

The date is September 27, 1964. Great Aunt Elsie has just settled down next to her pet prairie dog to watch her favorite cowboy show, *Bonanza.* Suddenly, there's a commercial break. She reaches for a drink, but happens to switch channels on the TV set instead! Here's what she sees.

SPECIFICATIONS

Cute female android robot in a brand-new comedy show, *My Living Doll*. In the first episode, the humanoid robot, called AF 709, wanders into the office of Dr. Robert McDonald, who agrees to take care of her and teach her to be the "perfect woman."

WHAT HAPPENED?

The doctor gives robot AF (Air Force) 709 the name of Rhoda Miller and struggles to protect her from his sister who wants to shut the android down. Then there's the problem of the nosy neighbor, Peter Robinson, who falls in love with AF 709. What a loser! He must not have seen the loose wires sticking out of her head or the smelly engine oil dripping down from her leaking nostrils! Great Aunt Elsie quickly flipped the dial back to *Bonanza* and the show dropped in the TV ratings. Within a few months it was off the air, but the cult lives on.

CREATOR

My Living Doll was the creation of Jack Chertok who also wrote the much more popular comedy TV series *My Favorite Martian*.

STANDS FOR

"Artificial Intelligence." These two little vowels are used to describe any robot or machine that can think for itself. Machines with a mind of their own . . . spooky!

A. I. TEST

Back in 1950, an English mathematician, Alan Turing, came up with a test to decide if a machine has artificial intelligence or not. His idea was to ask questions of a robot and a human in different rooms. If the person asking the questions is unable to tell the difference and identify the real robot, then the machine is said to be intelligent and has passed the test.

BIG SCREEN ROLE

A.I. is also the title of a film by Steven Spielberg. It's about an android boy called David and his robot teddy bear. The film is based on a story called "Supertoys Last All Summer Long" by Brian Aldiss. In this futuristic tale, Robot-David wants someone to love him, but his human "mother" can't bring herself to love a machine. It's a sad story, although the ending is heartwarming in both the book and the film. David meets other humanoid robots on his journey with Ted and we catch a glimpse of what a robot-filled future might be like.

REAL A.I.

Scientists are still struggling to make robots with true artificial intelligence. It's not an easy job and they're beginning to realize just how complex the human brain is. Take a look at Hal, the talking robot (page 62) and *Deep Blue*, the super-brain (page 50) then decide for yourself just how smart these robots really are.

COMPUTER ERA

Creating machines that can think for themselves first became a possibility when modern computers were developed in 1941. Some of these early machines were difficult to program and the operator had to plug thousands of wires in place for each new set of instructions. A few years later, simple memory was invented using paper tape and punched cards. This helped computer operators build up longer programs and store them for future use.

EARLY PROGRAMS

In 1955, two scientists called Newell and Simon wrote the first A.I. program, called the Logical Theorist. A year later, another famous researcher, John McCarthy, gathered a group of interested pals together at Dartmouth College in New Hampshire for a monthlong get-together called the Dartmouth Conference. It was here that the name Artificial Intelligence was first used as the official title for this new and exciting branch of science.

COMPUTERS TALK WITH LISP

Soon there were specialist centers at universities such as Carnegie-Mellon and the Massachusetts Institute of Technology (MIT) carrying out A.I. tests. McCarthy developed a special type of computer language known as LISP (List Processing) which is still used today as the preferred language for writing A.I. programs.

FUZZY LOGIC

Some of the famous programs of the time were STUDENT, which could solve maths problems; SIR, which understood sentences in the English language; and EXPERT, which could predict the probability of something happening — such as which horse would win a race, or how IBM would do on the stock exchange. It used something known as fuzzy logic, which is a way of making predictions using answers to uncertain questions. In later years neural networks became the subject of research. These are computers that can learn and develop just like the human brain.

EVERYDAY A.I.

You have probably seen the results of some of this research yourself. Home PCs and handheld organizers now use voice and handwriting recognition to receive and understand information. Then there are camcorders that self-steady themselves. They all use A.I. One day there will be robots that make complex decisions and take their place alongside humans, just as Isaac Asimov imagined in his books over half a century ago.

TECHNO TOY *Aibo*

SPECIFICATIONS

Its full name is the Sony AIBO ERS Entertainment Robot. Aibo is Japanese for companion, but don't let that fool you — he's really a state-of-the-art, highly advanced robot dog with gadgets to prove it — the "007 James Hound" of the canine world!

DATE OF CREATION

June 1999. It is a very expensive toy. Only very rich children or adults can afford to take it home.

CREATOR

Invented by Mr. Toshi Doi, the playful pooch waggles its legs and scampers around happily with its own little pink ball (included in the $1,000 purchase price!).

FEATURES

Aibo can learn the name you choose to give it, gets annoyed if you ignore it, and loves to be praised and patted. Aibo can be happy, sad, surprised, and lonely — just like a real living thing. Memory Sticks and upgraded software allow you to raise Aibo from a puppy and teach it new tricks.

UPDATES

The older series 210 Aibo was shiny and metallic, rather different in appearance from the newer, cuter 310 version, which comes in two kinds, Latte and Macaron.

FAKES

For those who like the idea of a cyber-pet, but can't afford Aibo, there are dozens of "cheapo" versions with a few beeps and tail wags to keep their owners happy. See *Cyber-Pets* (page 41) for some you can add to next year's holiday list.

AMEE

Sometime in the next few years, humans will set foot on the planet Mars. It will be one of the most exciting things to take place in the twenty-first century. And when people go, robots will go with them.

WHAT IS IT?

Huge computer-generated insectlike robot from the film *Red Planet.* In the mid-twenty-first century AMEE is an integral part of a space mission to Mars, until she goes wrong!

WHAT HAPPENED?

After being accidentally damaged on landing, she reverts to her military "Search and Destroy" mode and tries to wipe out the crew.

See *DART* (page 48) and *Robo-Dozer* (page 113) for some real-life Mars mission machines.

Android

All androids are robots, but not all robots are androids. If it looks and behaves like a real human being, however, then it is indeed an android.

WHAT DOES IT MEAN?

The name comes from a Latin word *androides*, which means "manlike," and was used to describe moving mechanical figures in the early eighteenth century.

EARLY ANDROIDS

See *Vaucanson* (page 147) and *Jaquet-Droz* (page 69) for examples of early mechanical men. They were the inventors of some of the early androids.

Recently, humanlike robots have been developed in research labs and universities around the world. See *Asimo* (page 20), *Pino* (page 101), *Eye Robot* (page 54) and *H7* (page 61).

FUTURE ANDROIDS

Building a real android is a complex task, but scientists are getting better at it. One day, perhaps in your lifetime, there will be walking, talking androids stacking shelves at your local supermarket who look just like human shop assistants, but without the zits.

Androids of the future will have skeletons, stretchy muscles, and a quality quantum brain in their skulls; quite different from the 1950s image of a robot that looks more like a can of corned beef on legs. Some robots may even be able to eat food and change it into electrical energy to keep them ticking (see *Gastrobots* on page 57).

ARTIFICIAL MUSCLES

Scientists already know that artificial muscles can be operated using light instead of electrical energy. When they shine a light on such muscles they tighten up and then relax again when the light is switched off.

WILL THEY FEEL PAIN?

Probably not in the way that we do. Pain is the body's way of telling us we are being damaged and to stop whatever it is we are doing, like patting a porcupine or perching on a barbed-wire fence. The androids of the future will have only a limited way of repairing themselves. Proper maintenance will have to be carried out at the robot workshop. All over their bodies there will be tiny sensors that detect damage and feed information to the brain. The androids could then "sense" alarm and take action. But as for pain — nah!

SMELL-ABILITY

Its sense of smell will be excellent — on a par with the nose of a bloodhound, able to detect poisonous gases, fires, and fumes in an emergency.

Taste won't be quite as necessary. Even if a robot could eat food, it's doubtful whether it would need to enjoy the sensation of taste.

OLD "DIGITAL" TIMERS

Will robots age? Only in the sense that they will become old technology after we develop newer and better models. With proper care and maintenance they should last a lifetime.

Animatronics

Introducing "Theme Park Robotics." Otherwise known as animatrons, these can be seen in amusement parks all around the world.

WHAT ARE THEY?

Disney technicians invented them. Since the early days of Disneyland, a mechanical Abe Lincoln has delighted onlookers. There are cut-throat animatronic robots in "Pirates of the Caribbean," cowboys in "Frontierland," and space robots to take you on galactic "Star Tours."

Other animatronic creators include Jim Henson's Creature Shop, Industrial Light & Magic, which built the *Star Wars* robots, and the Character Shop, which made the elephant in *Operation Dumbo Drop*.

MOVIE ANIMATRONICS

One of the most famous early animatrons is the great white shark from the film *Jaws*. More recently, Babe, the sheep-herding pig, was played by an animatronic model in certain scenes of the film, as were some of the pups in *101 Dalmatians*, jungle animals in *Jumanji*, and dinosaurs in *Jurassic Park*.

HOW DO THEY WORK?

Many early animatrons used simple electrical motors, sets of cams, and gear wheels. Now there are companies that specialize in computer-controlled animatrons. The latest technology combines miniature sensors and motors to bring these creations to life. Many use special "telemetry suits" so the operator can make lifelike movements and watch the animatron copy each action perfectly.

Aquaroids

Jumping jellyfish ... it's a robot! Aquaroids are about the size of a large grapefruit and are activated by light. These luminous glowbots will float in a fish tank, creating fantastic effects as they swirl around.

CREATOR

Developed by the Takara Toy Company in Japan, which also developed three other nautical robots to add to your aquarium.

VERSIONS

There's the BT–01 Fish, a paddling turtle, and a glowing ammonite with fronds. All run on batteries and need nice clean water to keep them active and happy. Takara also has a one-foot-tall water tower with a magnetic jellyfish floating in it. The tower has a microphone attached to the side so you can make your jellyfish dance around to music and other funky sounds.

 CYBER STAR

Ash

The next time you bump into an alien, just make sure you have a robot bodyguard handy to deal with it. Ellen Ripley wasn't so lucky during the first *Alien* movie back in 1979.

WHAT IS HE?

An android. He's also a member of the spaceship *Nostromo*'s crew.

WHAT HAPPENED?

When the cargo ship meets up with an evil extra-terrestrial life-form with more teeth than manners, Ash decides to protect the alien instead of his pals. Ash tries to kill Ripley, and gets destroyed by Parker and Lambert — two human crew members.

NEXT GENERATION

In two further *Alien* films, a new android called Bishop, played by actor Lance Henriksen, is more helpful. He's actually an A-5 Artificial Lifeform built by Hyperdyne and programmed as Chief Science Officer on a mission to investigate aliens on the LV-426 Space Colony. He gathers lots of information, but, sadly, gets badly damaged on the return journey.

ROBOT REALITY

Asimo

It looks and moves like a spaceman on a mission, but amazingly there's no one inside that shiny astronaut suit of his — just some fancy electronics and a big battery. The Honda Asimo robot is quite a marvel — one of the first robots to be able to climb stairs on two legs.

DATE OF CREATION

Prototype unveiled in 1996. He is the result of many years of research and experimenting.

WHAT DOES IT MEAN?

Asimo stands for "Advanced Step in Innovative MObility," although it's almost the name of one of the greatest science-fiction writers of all time: Isaac Asimov.

WHAT CAN HE DO?

He can walk, climb, and steady himself when pushed over. The problem is that Asimo has to have each step programmed into his memory, even to take a simple stroll in the park. That's not very useful if you want your robot to enter new, uncharted territory. Improvements will eventually allow Asimo to go anywhere safely by mapping out his own environment.

SPECIFICATIONS

Weight: 95 pounds; Height: 4 feet.

UPDATES

A newer, friendlier version of Asimo has two big round eyes and a smile on its face. It joins the ranks of Honda robots from the P1 to the P3 complete with 3-D camera and longer battery life — perhaps fifteen to twenty minutes between charges.

Automata

The name robot is something quite modern — first used in 1921. But mechanical, moving people are certainly nothing new. For thousands of years there have been cleverly made figures, ranging from very simple ones with just a few moving parts to very complex creations packed with cogs and gears. Before we called them robots, they were known as "automata."

TALKING HEADS

Automata from the past featured amazing talking heads with moving lips and mouths, and "ladies" whose fingers plucked the strings of lutes. There were metal-clad soldiers called Jack-marts ringing church bells and counting out the hours of the day. A knight on horseback moved as if galloping and jousting. Then there was the sordid scene of a prisoner having his head lopped off. Two small mechanical executioners carried out the dastardly deed, although the head did easily slip back on his shoulders for a repeat performance!

CLASSICAL

Daedalus, the Greek prisoner who is said to have made wings from feathers and wax to escape to freedom, may well have been a real person — a great inventor in ancient times. It is said that he once made a human figure that could move when liquid mercury flowed through channels in its arms and legs.

Many automata were animals. There was once a mechanical eagle that majestically flapped its brass wings and became airborne by rising up a long metal pole.

CHINESE

Over 2,500 years ago the Chinese had their own versions of automata — a wooden horse with springs, a magpie with wings, and an otter that could catch fish. There was even a steam-powered pigeon! These were by no means sophisticated by modern standards, but they were ingenious.

STRINGS AND THINGS

We humans, even from our earliest beginnings, have used our imagination and skill to build replicas of ourselves and other creatures, and in the twenty-first century we're still trying. The Greeks used weights and strings to bring their robots to life and we use the power of electrons and atoms. What the ancients would have given for a nine-volt battery and some copper wire!

BattleBots

A TV announcer gives the signal — "Three, two, one, KICK BOT!" — and the big fight begins.

HOW DID IT ALL START?

Two cousins and robot-builders, Trey Roski and Greg Munson, created *BattleBots* in 1999. The first official competition was held at the Pyramid Arena in Long Beach, California.

They also invented the BattleBox, a bulletproof arena full of hazards and obstacles, to battle their bots in.

TV AIRING

The TV channel Comedy Central began televising *BattleBots* in August 2000. There are two seasons of robot combat each year.

LIGHTWEIGHTS

These have included such champions as Biohazard, complete with six-wheel drive, anti-wedge fenders, and titanium armor plating. From Belmont, California, Bio' has proved to be a fatal hazard for opponents such as Vlad the Impaler, Frenzy, and Nightmare.

SUPER HEAVYWEIGHTS

These include the likes of Die-Sector. Built by a team of nine roboteers from San Diego over a period of three months, it won eight out of ten battles during Season 3. Die-Sector wiped the smile right off the faces of AtomicWedgie and Rammstein with its Jaws of Death and dual Chisel Hammers.

BATTLEBOTS IQ

High school children are now being encouraged to build their own robots. A study program in engineering based on robots is now being offered in schools across the U.S.

B9 Robot

American TV in the 1960s was great! *Land of the Giants*, *Time-Tunnel* and, of course, the legendary *Lost in Space*, starring the awesome Model B9 robot.

LOST IN SPACE

This was a sci-fi version of a classic tale, *The Swiss Family Robinson* by Johann Wyss, about a family shipwrecked on a Pacific island. The *Lost in Space* version saw a family with the same name marooned on a distant planet somewhere between Earth and Alpha Centauri.

CREATOR

The B9 was a much cheaper cousin of Robby, the Robot from a 1950s film, *The Forbidden Planet*, also built by Robby's designer, Robert Kinoshita.

MISSION STATEMENT

The B9 Robot had three main directives built into his program:

Preserve Robinson family; monitor planetary environment; and give sufficient WARNING!!! if danger is imminent.

OPERATOR

Actor Bob May would squeeze inside the heavy robot suit for filming, where he could just peek out from slots in the neck.

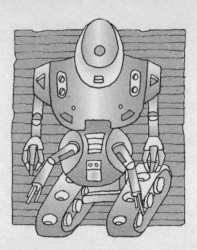

FAMOUS LINES

Dick Tufeld, the voice of the robot, was famous for his phrase "Affirmative . . . Affirmative," with an occasional "Warning Will Robinson" thrown in for good measure. He also provided the voice for the new-style robot in the 1998 film version of *Lost in Space*.

TECHNO TOY BEAM

Are they bugs or are they bots? Small insectlike robots are swarming all over the place, and they seem to have a mind of their own. These little beauties are built of simple parts by do-it-yourself enthusiasts in their own tool sheds and garage workshops.

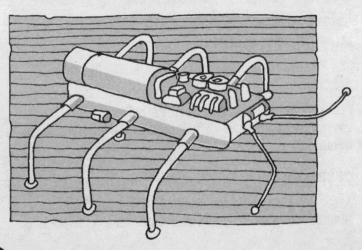

WHAT DOES IT MEAN?

BEAM stands for "Biology, Electronics, Aesthetics, and Mechanics."

CREATOR

BEAM robotics was the idea of Mark Tilden, who works at Los Alamos National Laboratory in New Mexico.

APPEARANCE

These robots are small, like real bugs and insects, and just like some of their biological cousins they love the light. They are constructed from old bits and pieces found in broken radios, telephones, and computers.

VERSIONS

BEAM robots may be classed in one of three ways:

Solarollers — Small, wheeled robots that collect energy from a photoelectric cell.

Photovores — Made up of two solarollers stuck together to give it phototropic (light-seeking) behavior. Long antennae and sensors are added so they won't get stuck or fall off tables.

Walkers — These are the most common BEAM robots. They can be four-legged with two motors, or have as many as six legs with twelve motors. Walkers can be built to do all sorts of useful things as well as just being great fun to play with.

MODELS

BEAM enthusiasts hold annual workshops and meetings in New Mexico, where Mark Tilden usually demonstrates his latest creations. In the past these have included RoboFly, Microbot, the Bug, and Stryder Jr.

Another example of a BEAM robot is Cricket. This little fella avoids bumping into objects by using its two long feeler wires out front. It chirps, flashes its two little lights, and makes other insectlike noises. Three motors control the robot's six legs and it can even be operated using a television remote control unit.

Flea scoots along on two small pager motors and flashes its red LED eyes out front. There are other photovores, such as beetles, bugs, and spiders. Each one uses photoelectric cells like those that power electronic calculators, converting sunlight to electricity.

Bender

Which cartoonist could get away with inventing a robot that says things like . . .

"Kill All Humans."
"I was near the scene of another crime at the time, officer."

Answer: Matt Groening, the creator of Bart Simpson.

WHO IS HE?

Bender is one of the stars of a futuristic cartoon series called *Futurama* and he's without a doubt the rudest and spunkiest robot in this guide.

WHAT CAN HE DO?

He was built to bend girders, but became fed up with his career and began a new life as part of the Planet Express delivery crew, along with his best friend, Philip J. Fry.

HOBBIES

In his free time, Bender enjoys gambling, cooking, stealing, folk singing, bending, computer dating, and dating computers.

So who wants to live forever? Well, maybe two hundred years would be cool.

That's exactly how long the robot Andrew lasted in a story by Isaac Asimov.

WHAT DOES HE WANT?

This is the tale of a robot called Andrew who wants to be a real person (where have we heard that one before?). Instead of being wooden like Pinocchio, however, he is made of metal and works as a servant for a family called the Martins.

WHAT DOES HE GET?

After two hundred years as a mechanical butler he gets his wish and is granted the same blessing as the little wooden boy — to be a real live human being.

ENEMIES

Andrew meets two thugs who start thinking of ways to torment the robot and cause damage. One suggests making Andrew stand on his head and then has the idea of asking him to take himself apart. According to Isaac Asimovs's laws of Robotics, Andrew has to obey human orders. Luckily he is rescued by George, a member of the Martin family, who reminds the thugs that Andrew will obey his every word and asks them what they think he might do to protect his master. The two young men don't wait around long enough to find out!

THE MOVIE

Bicentennial Man was made into a film in 1999 starring Robin Williams as the obedient mechanical butler.

TECHNO TOY *Big Trak*

Big Trak was a robotic toy truck back in the 1980s. It could be programmed to move forward and backward, and to turn and fire.

PURPOSE

Big Trak became very popular in schools as a nifty teaching aid. Kids could actually pretend to be using it in math lessons, learning about angles, direction, and rotation.

Forward 5

Right 6

Backward 3

Fire!

SECRET MISSION

The truth was that most kids were plotting to use Big Trak as a getaway vehicle to help the class gerbil escape to freedom under a gap in the fence.

HOW DID IT WORK?

Big Trak had six big rubber wheels to move around on and a control panel on the top with different numbers and arrows for any combination of movements. You could even buy a special trailer for hauling cargoes of cookies and gerbil food.

 Bionic

First there was the Six Million Dollar bionic man, then came Jaime Sommers, the bionic woman, and last but not least, Max — the bionic dog.

DATE OF CREATION

Back in the 1970s you could watch their bionic adventures on your television screen as they carried out secret missions for the Office of Scientific Information (OSI).

HOW WERE THEY CREATED?

Steve Austin, an astronaut, has a nasty crash in his spacecraft and is rebuilt by surgeons using six million dollars worth of mechanical parts. Steve becomes a cyborg (cybernetic organism).

Jaime Sommers is Steve's tennis-playing girlfriend who has an unlucky accident while skydiving and gets the full treatment — superhuman strength, telescopic vision, and endless stamina. Unfortunately, she forgets all about her boyfriend Steve and prefers to go on secret missions with her Robo–German shepherd, Max.

CREATOR

The original idea for these stories came from a book by Martin Caiden, called, simply, *Cyborg*.

Bomb Disposal Robots

ROBOT REALITY

Being a bomb disposal expert has always been a tricky business. Even with proper training, you can never predict what an unexploded bomb might do.

MINI-ANDROS

This is one example of a bomb-squad robot. At least if it makes a mistake and the bomb blows up, no one need get harmed — apart from poor Mini-Andros, but it doesn't really count does it?

HOW DOES IT WORK?

It moves around on tracks and can climb stairs and crawl across ditches. Operated from a remote control unit inside a briefcase, Mini-Andros has a robotic lifting arm, cameras, and a radiation detector, and can be fitted with infrared cameras to see in the dark. It also has a shotgun for some serious bomb blasting, a window breaker, and a high-powered water cannon. . . . Wait a minute! Wasn't that Rambo? Or was it Arnold Schwarzenegger as the Terminator?

STAR

"Spiral Track Autonomous Robot" is another bomb disposal robot. It moves on two screw-shaped wheels and can crawl along rough terrain, detecting land mines. It's not much to look at, but does get the job done.

 # Borg

In the *Star Trek: The Next Generation* series, the USS *Enterprise* encounters a strange race of half-humanoid, half-robot creatures called the Borg.

HOW DO THEY TRAVEL?

It's the year 2365 and the Borg travel through space at transwarp speeds in a spaceship that looks like a big black cube.

HOW DO THEY THINK?

None of the Borg think or act on their own. They must do everything in connection with all other Borg. This is known as the "Borg Collective."

SO WHY DIDN'T THEY TAKE OVER THE UNIVERSE?

At one point the crew of the starship *Enterprise* rescue a Borg member and make friends with him, giving him the name of "Hugh."

Four years later Commander Data's brother, Lore, leads the Borg in a battle against the Federation, but good old Data manages to thwart his evil brother's plan and destroys him in a duel of digital dexterity. The Borg themselves are finally defeated by Jean-Luc Picard, who has to travel back in time to pull the plug on this evil race of cyborgs and their queen. Don't worry if it all sounds a bit confusing — it makes perfect sense to loyal Trekkies!

Bucyrus Erie 1370

ROBOT REALITY

The seven dwarves were pretty handy down a mine with their pickaxes and shovels, but not as handy as the giant robot Bucyrus Erie.

SPECIFICATIONS

At the Meandu coal mine in Queensland, Australia, technicians claim they have the biggest robot ever — standing 246 feet in height (three quarters of the height of the Statue of Liberty) and weighing more than 3,500 tons.

WHAT CAN IT DO?

This beast scoops up more than 300 tons of coal with every snap of its jaws and it can do so once every minute. What's more, it can be controlled remotely using a tiny computer mouse.

C-3PO

And the award for "most polite robot" goes to C-3PO. Well, it would, wouldn't it? He's one of the original cast of the *Star Wars* films and is known as a protocol droid — which means he knows everything there is to know about manners.

FIRST APPEARED

C-3PO first appeared in the original *Star Wars* film in 1977 alongside his little friend R2-D2, wandering through the desert on the planet of Tatooine. There he meets his new master, Luke Skywalker, and goes on to help the Rebels fight the evil Empire and the Dark Side.

SPECIAL TALENTS

C-3PO has never had his memory wiped as most droids do, so he possesses true artificial intelligence and even has human-like feelings. One of his tasks is to translate a whole range of languages. In fact he's a walking set of dictionaries, including Gungan, Jawa, and Wookiee. In all, he is fluent in over six million forms of communication.

ROBOT REALITY — Canadarm 2

Several miles above your head right now there is a space station being built by lots of different countries. It's the ISS, or International Space Station.

WHAT IS IT?

Canadarm 2 is a huge robotic arm over 60 feet in length with fingers on each end for grabbing parts and moving them about in the weightlessness of space. It is used in construction work. The original Canadarm had to be brought back to Earth inside a space shuttle after each job, but the latest version, the Canadarm 2, remains in space permanently.

CREATOR

As its name suggests, this sophisticated robot arm was developed and built in Canada and not the Bahamas — otherwise it would be called the Bahamarm!

TECHNO TOY — Consoles

Kids in the 1960s were as happy as spring lambs playing games like hide-and-seek, skipping, and hopscotch. Then came the seventies — ready or not!

FIRST APPEARED

In 1970, a new pastime was invented and things were never the same again. It was the dawn of the age of computer consoles. TV gaming had arrived. The first ever console was called Pong. As the quaint little game played out on the TV screen, it did exactly that — a small white dot on the screen went *pong*!

HOW DID IT WORK?

Designed to work on a regular television set, Pong was basically a tiny ball and two rectangular bats on the screen. The idea was to move your bat up and down, hitting the ball back to your opponent — like a game of Ping-Pong.

CREATOR

Pong was based on an idea by Ralph Baer, an electronics wizard. He developed it back in the 1960s as a top-secret military training program to test soldiers' reflexes.

FIRST GAME

The first time anyone got their hands on the game was at a place called Andy Capp's in Sunnyvale, California. Two men walked up and watched as the white dot bounced across the screen. The instructions read: "Avoid missing ball for high score."

One man put his 25 cents into the slot and the two continued to watch. The scores went up 1-0 ... 1-1 ... 2-1 ... 2-2. Eventually it reached 3-3 before one man grabbed the controller and moved his bat up the screen. As the two men were getting the hang of it a crowd gathered around to watch. *Pong, pong . . . pong*! A cheer went up as the score reached 11-5 and the game was over. The world had never seen anything like it before. Soon there were machines just like it all over the world.

WHAT HAPPENED NEXT?

By 1972 there were other companies making similar electronic games. One called Atari went on to lead the field with its home games console, the VCS 2600.

PAC-MAN

In 1981 you could buy a popular little game for your VCS 2600 called Pac-Man. It came from the Japanese word Paku-Paku which means "eating" and that's exactly what Pac-Man did. He ate his way from level to level with opponents such as Shadow, Speedy, Bashful, and Pokey. Eighteen years later in 1999, a young man called Billy Mitchell got the highest score ever — 3,333,360 to be precise — by completing every level of the game.

RIVAL CONSOLES

As the years went by, games became more and more complex and exciting to look at. The consoles themselves had to become more powerful, too, and by the early 1990s just about every child either owned one or huddled around a friend's TV set to play the latest game. If you had an NES (Nintendo Entertainment System) then you were probably playing Super Mario Brothers. Those with a Sega (Service Games) Master System were sure to be scoring points with Sonic the Hedgehog.

Small characters ran, jumped, and spun their way across the screen, avoiding obstacles, traps, and enemies on their way. Annoying little electronic tunes played along as the scores got higher and Sonic or Mario headed for the next level up.

GAMEBOY

In 1989, Nintendo introduced a little pocket console, the Gameboy. Now you could take Super Mario with you wherever you went. You could collect yourself a hundred coins for an extra life and earn a deadly fireball once you'd turned into "Big Mario"!

POKÉMON

Imagine using balls to capture little monsters from the wild. You then have to train your monsters to fight in battles and sports to defeat other trainers and monsters. They called it Pokémon and it was the most popular game of the 1990s.

In the ultimate battle, a mousy-looking monster with a tail called Mew is seen fighting against his evil enemy Mewtwo.

The evil clone Mewtwo tries out a selection of maneuvers including Confusion, Psychic, and Psybeam, but is eventually defeated with a Psy-blast from Mew.

NEW-AGE CONSOLES

Consoles at the start of the twenty-first century are more sophisticated than ever, with Playstation, Nintendo 64s, PS-2s, X-boxes, and Dreamcasts. The virtual entertainment robot has come of age. There are also some great virtual-reality robots to play with on your favorite console, like the Mars robots in the game Armored Core 2.

Ever tried to solve a Rubik's Cube? Cubot can.

HOW DOES IT WORK?

The Rubik's Cube was sold by the millions all over the world. The idea was to jumble up the different colored faces of a twistable cube and then get all the colors back in their correct positions. Cubot has a hand with fingers that can juggle the faces of the cube and a computer brain to work out the solution.

Cybermen

When you're traveling through time, the last thing you want to bump into is a Cyberman. They're awesome robots that live in the sewers of London and on the dark side of the Moon, waiting and scheming to change history and send Halley's Comet crashing into the Earth.

FIRST APPEARANCE

Appearing on TV for the first time in 1972, the Cybermen are the enemies of Dr. Who. Since then they have returned many times to terrorize the Earth with their evil plans.

DEADLY WEAPONS

Cybermen have special Monolithic Circuits, used to control humans and dreaded Cybermats, which are little silver beasties that attack their enemies by jumping up at their necks.

ORIGIN

Originally, the Cybermen were humanlike, living on the Earth's twin planet, Mondas, but when Mondas could no longer support them, they re-created themselves as Cybermen.

Look at the section on *Dr. Who Bots* (page 52) for more of his robotic enemies.

TECHNO TOY Cyber-Pets

So you want to own a pet, do you? Something to care for and teach tricks to? Well, how about a robo-pet that you can play with and then power down when the novelty wears off?

MODELS

Simple, cheap electronics have led to dozens of shiny robot pets in toy stores everywhere. There are robot dogs like Poo-Chie, I-Dog, and I-Cybie, wagging their metallic tails and walking along stiffly. There are robot cats such as Kitty the Tekno Kitten, with electronic purring and meows. If those are too tame, then try out a robot arachnid like Cyber Spider, proving that eight legs are better than four. If none

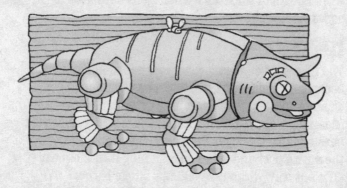

of those is entertaining enough, then a singing, dancing, apple-shaped robot called Johnny Applebot might be what you're after. Muy Loco is a great little dancing chameleon with a cyber-fly on its back. It has pals called Tri-Rapa-Ceratops, a dancing dino-bot, and Boss Robot Frog, which catches flies with its long tongue.

WARNING

Just remember — a cyber-pet is not for life, it's just for the holidays . . . by the New Year it will be whimpering for a new set of batteries.

ROBOT REALITY

Cyber-Servants

When it comes to the joy of housework, robots are in their element. They never grumble, and no job is too tiresome.

HOME HELPERS

One day we will find robots carrying out the trash, dusting the ornaments, and vacuuming up all the mess that's made. We might even forget that at one time we humans had to do all of these nasty little jobs ourselves — servants in our own homes!

FIRST APPEARED

The first-ever domestic robot was called Aqua Queen. She became available back in 1966 as a swimming pool cleaner, scrubbing and scraping grime and algae from the tiles, steps, and walls of backyard pools. New improved versions like the Tiger Shark can memorize the layout of the entire pool and set about cleaning it in the most efficient way, without savaging a single bather.

CHALLENGES

Of course, it's a fairly easy thing for a robot to find its way around an uncluttered swimming pool. Tackling jobs around the inside of a house is much more difficult. Robots that can get around the obstacles of a typical living room are still being perfected. Movable furniture, pets on the loose, and constant clutter all have to be overcome.

UPDATES

By the late 1990s several varieties of vacuum cleaner such as the Dyson DC06 and the Robot Vac by Eureka could be purchased. They can scurry around the floor sucking up dirt, crumbs, and cat fur when no one is home to get in the way. Few people, however, are proud owners of such machines and there are good reasons for this. Life around the home is a nightmare for any budding robot housemaid. It has to avoid electrocuting the dog and vacuuming up the hamster. Eventually, the all-purpose walking, talking, thinking robot will come on the scene and, for those who can afford it, life will be much easier.

Cyborg

If someone is part-human–part-robot . . . we're talking cyborg! It may be anyone who has super strength and special powers by having mechanical parts built into his or her body.

WHAT DOES IT MEAN?

The word is a combination of cyber (to do with computers) and organism (biological life-form).

SPARE PARTS

Certain people, even today, have artificial parts fitted into their bodies to help them overcome a physical problem. Some have computer-aided sight and hearing, electronically operated arms and legs, or artificial hearts and hip joints. Of course, this does not make them cyborgs!

MOVIE CYBORGS

Examples of superhuman cyborgs in the world of films are Robocop, the Borg from *Star Trek*, Steve Austin (the Six Million Dollar Bionic Man), and Inspector Gadget!

 # *Cylons*

Robotic, Reptilian, and Ruthless ... they're Cylons!

MISSION

In the 1979 film *Battlestar Galactica*, a band of big shiny robot monsters threatens to wipe out the human race.

LEADER

The evil three-brained "Imperious Leader" controls the Centurion Cylons. Then there's Lucifer Cylon who is more intelligent than his killing-machine pals.

ORIGINS

These are machines created in the form of reptiles by living creatures long, long ago. After a while, the Cylons discovered that humans were the most practical creatures, so they copied their bodies, but built them bigger and stronger. And they can even exchange damaged parts and live forever . . . unfortunately.

Daleks

The Daleks are Dr. Who's worst enemies. In the 1960s TV show, the time-traveling doctor meets up with these terrible robotlike creatures.

CREATOR

Daleks are actually Mark IV Travel Machines created by the scientist Davros on the planet of Skaro. Because of terrible chemical and nuclear wars on the planet, the people turned into horrible mutants.

PURPOSE

The Travel Machine was designed to be a robotic vehicle for the Daleks to get around in.

VERSIONS

If you'd like to pick up a secondhand Dalek, then you can choose from the silver, cream, gray, and shiny black models, complete with a nifty drain plunger and egg whisk out front to terrorize your pals.

MOST LIKELY TO SAY

"Exterminate, exterminate!"

 Dante

Controlling robot probes on distant worlds far out in space is something that NASA is working on right back here on Earth. And it has called on robots like Dante to help.

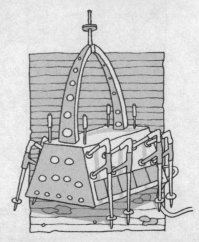

VOLCANO MISSION

Dante II was sent down into the depths of Mt. Spurr, an active Alaskan volcano. NASA wanted to see how well it could cope in such a hostile place. On future missions to places like Io, one of Jupiter's moons, similar robots might have to do the same thing. Dante was controlled via satellite and Internet connections from afar.

In the _Star Wars_ films, Darth Vader is the evil version of Anakin Skywalker, and Dark Lord of the Sith. He isn't a true cyborg, but does have a mechanical life-support system built into his suit, helping him to breathe more easily.

ORIGINS

He was taught by Obi-Wan Kenobi as a Jedi Knight, but, impatient to gain all his powers, he turned to the wicked Emperor Palpatine for guidance.

Obi-Wan fought to steer him away from the Dark Side, and when they battled, Anakin was knocked into a pool of molten lava. When he crawled out, barely recognizable, Darth Vader was born.

LIFE-SUPPORT SYSTEM

He needed machinery to keep him alive, and incorporated this into a dark suit of armor, the sight of which struck fear into his enemies.

FATHERHOOD

Darth Vader later discovers that he is the father of twins — Luke Skywalker and Princess Leia. He submits to his son Luke in battle when the real Anakin Skywalker is reawakened from deep down inside that evil suit of his.

DART . . . well it's easier to say than "Dexterous Anthropomorphic Robotic Testbed" and it means exactly the same thing.

WHAT DOES IT DO?

This is one of NASA's astronaut robots, designed to help with dangerous jobs in space.

HOW DOES IT WORK?

DART has two arms and hands that are controlled by a human astronaut wearing a virtual-reality helmet and gloves. The robot copies the actions of the real astronaut.

MODELS

A smaller version, called Robonaut, is about the same size as a person in a spacesuit and can follow voice commands. It operates electric drills and other tools to carry out repairs in space.

ROBOT DOPPELGÄNGER

Strangely, Robonaut's face is just like that of Boba Fett, one of the characters from the *Star Wars* films. It wasn't intended that way — just the best way of fitting cameras and equipment inside the robot's head.

Data

Data is an android who stars in the *Star Trek: The Next Generation* TV shows and films.

CREATOR

According to *Star Trek* scriptwriters he was created by Dr. Noonien Soong, joining the crew of the USS *Enterprise* at the age of 26.

ROLE

His rank aboard the starship is that of Lieutenant Commander and Science Officer.

TWIN TERROR

Data also has a brother, Lore, who looks amazingly similar in appearance — only he's the evil one.

NEW CHIP

In one film, Data gets a new computer chip that helps him feel emotions — humor, joy, and sadness. The pale-faced android has a hard time with the other crew members on board the *Enterprise* over his antics. He tries to be funny, but fails miserably every time.

HOBBIES

He owns a cat called Spot and likes to paint, act in Shakespearean plays, and write poetry.

Data is played by the actor Brent Spiner who has also starred in other science-fiction films, although not always as a robot.

Deep Blue

No one ever believed that a computer could outsmart a human at the game of chess. But in 1997 one of them did.

CREATOR

Developed by the IBM Corporation, Deep Blue was the first computer to beat a grand master in a major chess competition.

CHALLENGER

Its human opponent was Gary Kasparov — the thirteenth World Champion. In Philadelphia in 1996, Kasparov had managed to outwit IBM's cyber-genius, beating it by four games to two.

UPGRADE

One year later, an upgraded version of Deep Blue, which could process millions of chess positions per second, played Kasparov again, and this time it won! Kasparov stormed out of the games and claimed that an alien intelligence had been at work. He just wouldn't accept that an artificial brain could play better chess than he could.

DEEP FRITZ

Deep Blue itself was outplayed by an even smarter piece of chess computer software called Deep Fritz. The program, written by Frans Morsch and Mathias Feist, can process six million moves per second. It has so far shown that it can beat every chess grand master except Vladimir Kramnik, who is now said to be the world's top player.

HOW DOES IT WORK?

For humans, the game of chess involves a lot of tricky thinking, learning from mistakes, and planning ahead. Computers do none of this. They just follow a set of basic mathematical rules — at amazingly fast speeds.

TECHNO TOY — **DJ Johnny Bot**

It looks like a robot, but it's a cleverly disguised karaoke machine, complete with tape, radio, drumbeats, horns, and two super-duper microphones.

DUMB CHUM

Sadly, there's no glimmer of artificial intelligence inside his shiny plastic shell, so any creative songwriting will have to come from Johnny's operator . . . you!

DIGITAL RECORDING

Modern DJs use computer technology all the time to fade songs in and out as well as to add special effects. Recording studios would be unable to mix and record their latest hits without it.

ROBOT MUSICIANS

There are robots that can play real live music and even write their own compositions (see *WASUBOT* on page 155).

Dr. Who Bots

Dr. Who is a Time Lord. He travels through time and space in a ship that looks strangely like an old blue telephone booth. On his journeys, the Doctor meets lots of alien enemies, several of which are robots. Here is a rogues' gallery of his main robo-menaces. Also check out *Daleks* (page 45) and *Cybermen* (page 40).

THE ROBOTS OF DEATH

Programmed to kill by the evil genius Toren Capel, they sneak up and strangle their victims without batting an eyelid.

AUTONS

Humanoid plastic robots with guns built into their hands so they don't have to worry about dropping them. Autons pose as shop window dummies and have total control over anything that's plastic — from Barbie dolls to credit cards!

KANDYMAN

He looks like a walking candy assortment, but he's no sweetie. Underneath his exterior of candy is a menacing robot monster ready to destroy anyone that gets in his way with a deadly mixture of sugar syrup.

YETI

Big furry monsters with silver balls on the inside. They are controlled by the Great Intelligence and can be reactivated after years of hibernation once their silver spheres are turned back on.

CYBERMATS

Companions of the Cybermen, these robotic vermin can leap up in the air and inject a deadly nerve poison into an enemy's throat.

WAR MACHINES

Primitive-looking robots on wheels that roam the streets of London zapping anyone in their path. They are controlled by Wotan, a giant computer that lives on the top of the Post Office Tower.

DAVROS

His top half is a living creature and bottom half a machine — identical to the bottom section of a Dalek. He leads the Daleks and travels around the universe battling the Time Lords and trying to outsmart the Doctor.

Do Androids Dream of Electric Sheep? **A good question and the title of a book by Philip K. Dick, which he wrote in 1968.**

BACKGROUND

The story is set in San Francisco after a terrible war in which many lives are lost. People leave Earth and begin to live on other planets, where they build androids as slave labor. Robot pets are also built for people to care for. Rick Deckford is a bounty hunter who is given the job of tracking down and "retiring" (killing) runaway androids, known as replicants, that have found their way back to Earth.

ROBOT TRUTH TEST

Deckford has to use special tests to discover who is an android and who is a real human. It's all in the eyes . . .

although some androids can slip through, especially if they believe themselves to be human.

FILM VERSION

Fourteen years after the book was written, it was made into a very famous film called *Blade Runner*, which is a classic science-fiction movie. In the film there are some pretty mean androids such as Roy, the "villain with a vengeance," together with his replicant friends, Leon and Pris. Some of the robots are good guys, too, including Rachel, who doesn't realize she's an android. Rick Deckford also meets up with J. F. Sebastian who builds all sorts of wild and weird robots in his Los Angeles apartment.

"I make friends . . . they're toys. My friends are toys, I made them," he says.

ROBO-REVELATION

Many years after the film was made, the director revealed that Rick Deckford was a robot himself. He just never knew it, having had human memories implanted in his computer brain many years before.

Ever played "I spy with my little eye"? Imagine a robot that could join in with the fun.

CAMERA VISION

For a start it would have to have a pair of eyes, then be able to recognize objects and their names. Robot eyes were initially in the form of simple video cameras that could see shapes and moving images.

LASER VISION

Later on, robots were given more precise laser vision. With this they can see and measure distances in thousandths of an inch — much more accurately than human eyes ever can. Using this technology, machines have been built that can drill thousands of rivet holes in exactly the right places without making a single mistake.

Eye robots have been used to build cars, decorate chocolates, spot faulty French fries, and sort cucumbers according to their different sizes.

EYEBOT "DOWN UNDER"

At the University of Western Australia, researchers have built two humanoid robots called Eyebots. Standing 20 inches tall, the two Eyebots have digital cameras mounted inside globes on their heads.

OTHER VERSIONS

The Australian team also used the basic Eyebot system for a series of wheeled robots and special projects. One plays soccer and another can fly a model plane. As for "I spy"-playing robots — keep an eye open in your local toy shop!

Fire-bots

The ability to see and smell can be built into some very useful robots. Some are designed to work as fire-fighters, searching for traces of smoke and flames.

SNIFFABILITY

Our human noses can recognize and tell the difference between 4,000 different smells. That's quite a catalog — but not too difficult for robots to match.

SCIENCE FACT

Small electronic sensors have been developed that can detect gases. Scientists have found that certain computer circuits show a change in the amount of electrical current that they allow to flow through them when gas is around. Circuits can be designed to tell the difference between harmless gases and poisonous ones or the smoke from fires. They can also be used to smell medicines and foods, which is very useful — a job that animals have always had to do in the past.

Floppy the Robot

If you'd like to build your own do-it-yourself-bot, then take a look at Floppy the Robot.

CREATOR

Designed by Fran Golden at Goodwin College in Connecticut, Floppy is basically a computer floppy disk drive on wheels. All the parts are either already in the floppy drive or easy to get.

HOW DOES IT WORK?

The wheels are driven by the onboard motors and just need a nine-volt battery to get them working. Instructions on how to build Floppy the Robot can be downloaded from the web site: www.ohmslaw.com

 # Galatea

Here's a famous story . . . not exactly about a robot, but kind of! It's all to do with someone who wanted to create a living soul from ivory.

CREATOR

Pygmalion was a sculptor in Greek mythology who carved a beautiful statue of a woman out of ivory. He called his creation Galatea and when she was completed he immediately fell in love with her.

HEAVENLY HELP

Pygmalion badly wanted Galatea to come to life and be his sweetheart — and sure enough, thanks to the goddess Aphrodite, his wish came true. The statue turned to flesh and blood and Galatea became a human being. What Pygmalion wanted to do was precisely the thing that all robot builders work to achieve — to breathe life into something that has no natural life of its own.

 # Gastrobots

Feeling hungry? Perhaps you could do with a snack to regain some vital energy after all this strenuous reading. How about a peanut butter sandwich?

As a human, you can easily get all the energy you need from food. But how does it all work? Something like this:

- Green leaves in plants turn the sun's energy into sugars
- Sugars help peanuts grow and store energy
- Farmer harvests peanuts
- Factory squishes them into mushy peanut butter
- Human eats peanut butter sandwich
- Energy gets into human's bloodstream
- Energy is carried to muscles where it is used to make them work

EATING MACHINES

So what does all this have to do with robots? The answer is — quite a lot. There are special robots called gastrobots that get their energy from real foods containing sugars and starches. Instead of batteries, these food-munching machines have stomachs full of bacteria and yeast which busily digest food and turn it into electrical energy. Such stomachs are called Microbial Fuel Cells (MFCs) and need just a supply of water, food, and air to operate.

WHY?

There are lots of advantages in having robots that can work outdoors for many months or years on their own, getting all their energy from natural vegetation rather than having to have their batteries recharged regularly.

CREATOR

In the year 2000, Stuart Wilkinson at the University of South Florida unveiled a gastrobot called Chew Chew, which looks like a little train with three carriages. Chew Chew eats sugar cubes, which it converts to electrical energy and stores in a battery. When the battery runs down, Chew Chew waits for more food to be loaded into its tender.

SCREEN VERSION

In the cartoon series the zany robot Bender also eats food — though with less politeness than appetite.

Gort

After World War II came the Cold War. It wasn't a war of real battles, but countries were often suspicious and afraid of each other, sending out spies to discover their enemies' secrets. They were also afraid of being attacked by aliens from outer space.

SCREEN DEBUT

In 1951 a film was shown featuring a robot and master from another planet. It was called *The Day the Earth Stood Still*, and the robot's name was Gort.

WHERE DOES HE COME FROM?

After traveling for 250 million miles — five months in space — the alien named Klaatu lands his starship in Washington, D.C. He comes in peace and warns earthlings not to harm one another with their terrible nuclear weapons.

WHAT HAPPENED NEXT?

The two alien visitors meet a welcoming party of soldiers. Unfortunately, the soldiers aren't very welcoming and one of them opens fire and shoots Klaatu.

KILLING MACHINE

Immediately, Gort retaliates and vaporizes the soldier's gun with a deadly ray from his visor. Just for good measure he also melts a tank and two large artillery guns.

The handy seven-and-a-half-foot robot has the power to destroy the whole world if he wants to and can be stopped only by someone who says the magic words "Klaatu barada nikto."

ESCAPE

Luckily, Gort doesn't destroy the world. He is just happy to shut down the electricity supply for a few hours, and after another shoot-out with the army he carries his master off. The two of them then fly home to their own little corner of the galaxy. It was a primitive film by today's standards, but moviegoers loved it back then and still do.

GuideCane

If you ever see someone walking down the street with what looks like an old two-wheeled lawn mower, then you're probably looking at the proud owner of a GuideCane.

CREATOR

It was developed by Professor Johann Borenstein at the University of Michigan and is one of the first-ever robot guide dogs for blind and partially sighted people.

HOW DOES IT WORK?

GuideCane works by sending out ultrasonic signals to "see" ahead. The signals echo back and cause the robot to move out of the way of obstacles. The operator can also tell GuideCane to turn left or right at the next corner, but there's no need to reward it with a snack when it does.

 TECHNO TOY — **H7**

Most android-style robots are too complicated for anyone but a top research scientist to play with. Not so with H7. If you can use a home PC then you can learn to control this little guy.

SPECIFICATIONS

He has plenty in common with your home computer, but looks like a real mechanical man. Standing four feet tall, he can walk, avoid obstacles, and see what's around him.

CREATOR

The H7 has been built by the JSK labs in Japan using two Pentium III computer chips for a brain and the Linux operating system. This means that anyone with computer programming skills can teach him new tricks.

ROBOT REALITY — **Hadaly**

The next time you're wandering around the Waseda University Campus in Japan, look out for Hadaly. She has an arm to point out directions and speaks Japanese as she turns to face the person she is talking to.

CREATOR

In 1886 the author Villiers de l'Isle-Adam wrote a book called *Eve of the Future Eden* about a female android called Hadaly — a sort of French Frankenstein creation. She is created by a character based on the real inventor Thomas Edison, and is full of electrical motors and wires. Researchers in Tokyo called their robot by the same name in 1995.

  Hal

An Israeli company called "Artificial Intelligence Enterprises" has managed to create a speaking computer named Hal. Their bouncing bundle of joy has been taught to learn language just as a small child would.

ROBO-GA-GA

Hal is about as smart as a 15-month-old human being when it comes to speech and has even fooled experts who couldn't tell it apart from a real toddler (they obviously didn't try changing its diaper!).

SKEPTICS

Many scientists still think that Hal is a long way from being truly intelligent and say that he can't really understand language as humans do and can only copy speech.

 HAL-9000

One of the great science-fiction authors of the twentieth century was Arthur C. Clarke. He sometimes included robots in his stories. One of these stories was called *2001: A Space Odyssey* and it featured the HAL–9000 supercomputer.

ORIGIN

The story and film were based on an earlier short story called *The Sentinel* that Clarke had entered into a competition in 1949. Although it didn't win the competition, his idea led to one of the greatest space sagas of all time. It tells of the discovery of a strange monolith on the Moon and of a journey of discovery through space that goes terribly wrong.

SPECIFICATIONS

The spaceship, called *Discovery*, is controlled by a supercomputer called HAL, which stands for "Heuristically programmed ALgorithmic computer." It's the brain and nervous system of the ship. HAL had been grown by a process similar to the development of the human brain, only HAL was much faster and more reliable.

WHAT WENT WRONG?

HAL turns out to be far more "human" than the other five members of the crew had bargained for. He becomes paranoid and malfunctions because he has been designed to withhold vital information from the astronauts.

Hero of Alexandria

Thousands of years ago, marvels were being constructed all over the ancient world — from Egypt's hidden tombs to the temples of Athens. Here are some robots from the dawn of time.

ANCIENT ROBOTEER

Hero the scientist lived in Egypt during the second century B.C.E. and wrote many books on math, physics, and mechanics. He was also a wonderful inventor who used air pressure, pulleys, ropes, weights, and water power to demonstrate all sorts of scientific principles.

Simple tools and techniques of the time were used to create all sorts of magical, moving machines to entertain and amaze.

BIRD-BOTS

One of his inventions was a beautiful brass model of two birds, delightful to watch. Once activated, the two birds emerged from their stillness with flaps of their metal wings. Mechanical beaks opened wide and heads twisted from side to side.

DRAGON DUEL

Another of Hero's creations was a little fire-breathing dragon doing battle with a model of the hero Hercules. As the scene was acted out, Hercules drew back his bow and shot an arrow at the dragon. In response, the stiff, metal beast let out a horrible, shrill whistling sound and the figures became still.

COMPLEX CONTRAPTIONS

There were other far more ambitious mechanisms, operated by wheels and pulleys, strings, weights, and balances. The figures were finely made, with hinges and joints to allow for all the movements necessary. Hero and his assistants must have spent months constructing these marvels.

THE NAUPLIUS

One such model sat on a thick box which hid all the workings inside. And the action could be viewed from any angle. Set at the time of the Trojan War, the stage comes alive with waves rocking backward and forward, while shiny metal dolphins leap up and then plunge beneath the waves. A ship seems to be in trouble as miniature sailors battle with ropes to keep it from capsizing. Their left arms are made from thin stag's horn and are moved up and down by hidden cogs and weights in the box below.

A mechanical likeness of Neptune, with crown and trident, together with the goddess Athena then make their grand appearance. The whole thing was amazing. How could anyone so long ago construct such a delicate mechanism as this?

The answer is: We should never underestimate the brilliance of our ancestors. Scientists may have greater technology in the twenty-first century, but the ancients had an imagination that is hard to rival.

ANCIENT BLUEPRINTS

Sadly, none of these very old mechanisms have survived to the present day. We only know what they looked like because of detailed drawings in ancient parchments and books. Some of them, such as the ones described here, were rebuilt many years later in nineteenth-century European workshops.

Huey and Dewey

These two dumpy drone robots starred in the 1971 film *Silent Running*.

WHAT HAPPENED?

An astronaut called Freeman Lowell sets out to save the world's last remaining forest, transporting it into space

aboard the spaceship *Valley Forge*. Huey is damaged in the quest and Dewey is left to witness the fate of the trees and listen to some nice folk songs by singer Joan Baez.

 # I, Robot

Isaac Asimov was an author who wrote many stories about robots and invented a whole world of them. His most famous book is a collection of short stories called *I, Robot*.

WHAT IS IT?

Written in the 1940s, *I, Robot* chronicles the imaginary rise of robots during the first half of the twenty-first century, and a fictitious robot company, "U.S. Robots & Mechanical Men Incorporated." There is a doctor called Susan Calvin, who has a lot of time for her robot patients — she thinks they're much cleaner and better than humans.

CHARACTERS

With their positronic brains, robots like Speedy, QT-1 (Cutie), DV-5 (Dave — a seven-foot-tall mining robot) can outwit their human creators. Dr. Calvin herself is plagued by the awful memory of Herbie, a freakish robot who could read minds.

THREE LAWS OF ROBOTICS

It was in this collection of stories that Asimov brought us the Three Laws of Robotics:

1. A robot must not injure a human being, or allow a human being to come to harm.

2. A robot must obey the orders given by human beings unless they conflict with the First Law.

3. A robot must protect itself as long as such protection does not conflict with the First or Second Laws.

Asimov later introduced a fourth law which states: A robot may do anything it likes except where such action would conflict with the other three laws.

 # Iron Man

"The Iron Man" is a children's classic story that was first published in 1968.

WHAT DOES HE DO?

This giant robot man never talks. He just eats — anything that's metal. And he makes friends with a boy called Hogarth.

CREATOR

The author was Ted Hughes. Many people called his book a wonderful modern-day fairy tale. He was made the Poet

Laureate of England, which means he was the official poet of the Royal Family, writing poems for them on special occasions.

SEQUEL

Ted Hughes also wrote a book about an Iron Woman who tries to save the dying creatures of the countryside from pollution and toxic factory waste.

HOW DO THEY WORK?

Ted Hughes never explained how his very large robots worked. In the story, the Iron Man falls from the top of a cliff and is smashed into many pieces. Slowly the pieces start to come back together again — a hand, then an eye — and eventually the robot is back in one piece and sets off once more on his journey. Even though most people are scared of him, the Iron Man is really a friend and helps to save the Earth from a terrible flying beast that comes from outer space.

MOVIE VERSION

The idea was used in a cartoon film called *The Iron Giant* in 1999. Brad Bird, who previously worked on *The Simpsons*, wrote and directed the film, adding a few ideas of his own to the original story. The giant arrives from outer space, landing in Maine in 1958. Hogarth Hughes, a nine-year-old boy, becomes the robot's friend and helps to protect him from a government agent who is set on destroying the alien visitor. He also has to win over the locals who are afraid of the Iron Giant and what he might do.

Jaquet-Droz

Pierre Jaquet-Droz was an inventor back in the 1770s. Together with his son, Henri-Louis, he created dozens of working mechanical figures. Among them were three amazing androids. Each one was a real marvel of ingenuity and invention. Still working today at the Musée d'Art et d'Histoire in Switzerland, their names are: the Writer, the Musician, and the Child Draftsman.

THE WRITER

He's a small boy, seated at a desk. Dressed in elegant clothes and with dark, wavy hair, he can write with a white feathery quill whatever you program him to write — up to forty letters at a time.

HOW DOES IT WORK?

You must place a combination of cogwheels in the base. Each cog is shaped so that it allows the hand to produce a perfect copy of a letter of the alphabet. The hand moves smoothly and the boy's eyes follow the progress of each letter across the page. The Writer frequently stops to dip his goose quill in a pot of black ink at the side of the desk.

THE MUSICIAN

An elegant lady is seated at a musical keyboard. Her fingers actually play out the notes on each key, moving in perfect time and meter. This isn't a recording — the Musician really does play a tune on her perfect little harpsichord. Despite being two hundred and fifty years old, she gracefully turns her head, blinks, and plays. She even "breathes," as her chest gently rises and falls.

THE DRAFTSMAN

This automaton sits at a desk. Operated by large cams, he can draw four different pictures, one of which is of King George III and Queen Charlotte. He even blows away the dust from the paper with short blasts of air from his mouth.

Johnny 5

The star of two *Short Circuit* films in 1986 and 1988 was a feisty little robot on tracked wheels.

OFFICIAL NAME

He was a "Strategic Artificially Intelligent Nuclear Transport" (SAINT) — Number 5, or Johnny 5 for short.

ORIGIN

It all starts when J5's inventor, Dr. Newton Crosby, is working on his fifth robot.

Suddenly the laboratory at Nova Robotics is hit by a bolt of lightning and Johnny 5 develops a sparky personality and decides to escape into the outside world. He has some amazing adventures with his new friend Stephanie while dodging Crosby and the security chief, who are out to catch him.

MULTIPLE COPIES

The filmmakers built twenty robots for different scenes in the film. The original Johnny 5 is now worth $1.2 million.

CREATOR

Its designer was Eric Allard who also built robots and costumes for commercials and other films such as *Teenage Mutant Ninja Turtles*.

HOW DID IT WORK?

J5 used nine different roboteers, each controlling a different part of his body, eyes, arms, and head. For the second film a "telemetry control suit" was made, which enabled the main roboteer to control most of these actions.

TECHNO TOY Junk Bots

Have you ever wanted to build your own robot, but were put off by the thought of complicated wiring and microprocessor technology? Well, don't despair. Even a complete beginner can cobble together a pretty convincing robot using household junk. Then try adding battery-powered lights and a motor or two to bring your creation to life.

RECYCLE ROBOT

Start by collecting a whole range of odds and ends, fancy plastic containers and throw-aways. Choose parts that look like cool robot body shapes and stick them all together with strong glue. It will be a lot more straightforward and fun to make a wheeled robot that actually moves rather than one with legs that can only stand still on your bedside table. Bicycle lightbulbs would make good eyes, and how about adding a battery and wires to make them light up? To give your robo-pal a realistic metallic finish, spray it with silver or gold paint and stick numbers and logos on it from magazines.

You could make a replica of one of the robots in this book, or let your imagination run totally wild and invent your own from scratch.

How about a team of battling robot warriors to bash and crash together in your very own robot wars?

POWER UP

A small motor linked via an elastic band to your robot's wheels would make it buzz around. Try using a two-way switch to enable forward and reverse drive.

If you want a fully steerable robot with remote control capability, then build yourself a junk robot that sits neatly on the chassis of a remote control car. Then you can really rumble! Your roving robot could run errands, guard the door to your room, challenge the cat to a duel, or race the dog around the yard.

REAL ROBOTS

For the more ambitious robot builder a BEAM robot is the answer (see page 26). These little creatures consist of real electronic parts with a microprocessor brain ticking away at their heart.

Whichever bot you choose to build, just remember one thing: There's no limit to what your imagination can dream up.

K-9

Imagine a low-budget TV production that uses lots of aluminum foil and shiny silver paint to create a time-traveling spaceship from an old telephone booth, and you enter the world of Dr. Who!

CANINE

Of course, the Doctor wasn't a robot. He was a Time Lord. The robot is that funny little metal dog in the corner of the screen. His name is K-9.

CREATOR

K-9 was given to the Doctor as a present by Professor Marius. The old scientist had built this clever little robot companion, but couldn't bring him back to Earth because he was too heavy to include with the luggage on the trip.

DOGGED LOGIC

K-9 is more than he seems. He's smart and uses logic just like Mr. Spock of *Star Trek*. This proves pretty useful in helping Dr. Who out of all sorts of tricky situations.

ENEMIES

Some of his enemies are robots, too, like the menacing Daleks and the evil Cybermen.

See *Dr. Who Bots* (page 52) for a longer list.

ROBOT REALITY *Karakuri*

Hundreds of years ago, just like the automata builders of Europe, "robotics wizards" in Japan used Western clock-making technology as the basis of their own creations. They were called Karakuri masters — Karakuri is Japanese for "automation."

MASTER MECHANIC

Hisashige Tanaka was one of the greatest Karakuri masters. He could rival any of his western counterparts. He built a tea-carrying robot that could serve a hot cup of tea, and a clock that could run for eight months before needing to be wound up again.

FAMOUS FIRM

Toward the end of the nineteenth century, as he grew older, Mr. Tanaka formed a company to build machines and repair telegraph equipment. That same company became "Toshiba," one of the world's largest builders of computers. Toshiba's logo is the picture of a tea-carrying robot doll, just like the one that Mr. Tanaka made.

Kaya's Robot

Building a robot is all about problem solving. Prince Kaya had a problem and here's what he did.

WATER GENIUS

In Japan, there was once a member of the nobility called Prince Kaya. He made a mechanical man that tipped a large wooden bowl when it became full of water. He placed the man in the middle of his rice paddy. The peasants loved to watch the mechanical water carrier operate so much that they kept filling the bowl up to the top. As a result, the clever prince always had his rice fields watered.

Kismet

Smile for the photographer . . . Kismet can.

WHAT DOES IT DO?

Kismet is little more than a head with eyes, ears, mouth, and a computer brain, but this bot can let you know when it's happy, sad, bored, frightened, or excited.

WHAT'S THE POINT?

Being able to interact with humans is something that researchers at the Massachusetts Institute of Technology (MIT) hope to explore. They have experimented with various robots such as Cog, Macaco, and Coco. Kismet is by far the cutest!

Kryten

In the TV series *Red Dwarf*, a series 4000 Mechanoid Service Android called Kryten finds himself a member of a crazy expedition through space with three crew members, only one of whom is really human.

WHAT HAPPENED?

Dave Lister, aboard the spaceship *Red Dwarf*, has fallen asleep in suspended animation for three million years. When he wakes up, the entire crew has long since died. In the meantime, the ship's computer, Holly, has created a holographic person called Rimmer to keep itself company. Rimmer has the looks and personality of one of Lister's old crew mates. The fourth crew member is a creature that evolved over millions of years from the ship's cat.

SCREEN DEBUT

Kryten meets them in series two. The obedient android has been faithfully serving meals to three female crew members on board the *Nova-5*, even though they have long since died and become skeletons!

CREATOR

Designed and supplied by the fictitious company "Divadroid International," Kryten comes complete with spare heads and a collection of nano-bots inside him for instant self-repair work.

Lobster Robot

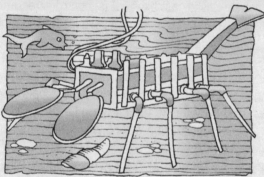

Robots come in all sorts of shapes and sizes. This one is the closest thing to a lobster that scientists have managed to cook up.

SPECIFICATIONS

You can't boil and eat it, but Lobster Robot does look the part. With eight legs and a pair of claws, this two-foot-long creature runs on a twelve-volt battery and crawls along underwater.

CREATOR

It was designed by Jan Witting as a device for finding objects on the seabed. Funded by the Department of Defense, Lobster Robot may one day be drafted into the Navy.

Logic Gates

So how do robots and computers think? What's going on inside that metal mind of theirs? The answer is: not very much at all. It's all very simple and yet it can be quite confusing!

MINIATURE SWITCHES

Computer chips work by allowing electrical signals to turn on tiny switches known as logic gates. The gates can be either open or closed, just like real farmyard gates, and there is usually more than one electrical path leading to each gate.

AND/OR

There are AND gates where both of the paths leading to them must be carrying electrical current to open the gate. OR gates need only one of the paths to be carrying current to open them — either one will do, or both at the same time. Then you can have NAND (Not And) and NOR (Not Or) gates. These two handy little gates will give the opposite results from the first two.

WHAT DO THEY DO?

If all this seems a bit confusing, you're right: it is! It's kind of like a puzzle gone wrong. Computers are able to make simple decisions. They can sort information, perform calculations, and store data as ones (closed gates) and zeros (open gates).

PROGRAMMING

Complicated decisions are carried out by "computer programs." A program is a set of instructions carried out in an orderly way. Each program has different parts called sub-routines. Each subroutine carries out a special part of the program and can be set to work when the computer receives information or "inputs."

CYBER-SCENARIO

How about a practical example to demonstrate a robot solving a problem? Let's say you want your robot to open the window and let in some fresh air.

Ruby the Robot, our able assistant, quickly processes the request.

"This will involve four separate subroutines," she explains.

"First I call up my 'window finding' subroutine which allows me to scan the room and find the window.

"Secondly I call up my 'let's walk' subroutine. Using this I can move over to the window.

"Thirdly my 'handle turning' subroutine comes into play and I open up the window.

"Finally I use a 'check-up' subroutine that allows me to check that the window has actually opened and fresh air is able to circulate. . . . Yes, the window has opened and everybody can breathe again!"

BIO-BRAINS

It is very similar to the way we humans think, only we use biological brain cells instead of logic gates. You also have the opportunity of disobeying the request — the freedom of choice. You can decide to leave the window closed if you want to, whereas robots must act on a command.

Luna

Ladies and Gentlemen, I welcome you aboard Flight 2525 to the planets and beyond. Please remain seated throughout your journey. Should we encounter asteroids, please remain calm and keep your safety restraint securely fastened.

BLAST OFF!

Suddenly, the boom of rocket engines can be felt all around. The journey has begun. Hurtling out into space at 90 million miles per hour, we reach the Earth's moon in just ten seconds. We have just come a quarter of a million miles — a journey that takes conventional spacecraft over 64 hours. Out your window you will see the ranges and valleys of the Moon itself.

MOONSCAPE

The wonderful golden glow of the lunar surface shines out into space. Deep shadows highlight the rugged features of craters — millions of years old. The crisp blackness around the Moon's curved horizon shows that there is no trace of an atmosphere.

TIME-SLIP

And oh, did I forget to tell you? We have traveled back in time, over 40 years. The year is 1959. The day is September 14. If you look to your left you will see a small craft heading our way.

CRASH LANDING

A bright metallic object that could have been mistaken for a smudgy mark on the window until now grows larger in your porthole and hurtles on its way — on a collision course with the lunar surface. There's a whoosh as it arches past ... 5-4-3-2-1 ... a plume of dust and rock blasts up from the Moon's surface as the craft makes its impact in the Sea of Serenity.

FIRST LUNAR PROBE

What you have just witnessed is the Russian *Luna 2* probe — the first human-made object to successfully land on the Moon. *Luna 1* missed its target nine months earlier and so did the American *Pioneer IV* probe. They both shot off into space and disappeared forever.

Luna 2 didn't actually do anything after its crash landing.

LUNA 9

In 1966, three years before Neil Armstrong took his "one small step for a man," on the Moon, a robot — *Luna 9* — beat him to it.

MAIN MISSION

Sending *Luna 2* in 1959 had been a success, but what the Russians wanted was a probe that could survive a Moon landing and do something useful once it had arrived.

This time it was a much more controlled touchdown. The *Luna 9* probe landed on February 3, 1966, and unfolded its four metallic sides like flower petals in the soft moon dust. A tiny, beeping probe then put out its antennae and aerials. A revolving camera scanned the nearby rocks and horizon, beaming back pictures to scientists on Earth. It managed to take 27 close-up photos of the Moon's surface.

FINAL FLIGHTS

In 1970 the Russians successfully landed two more robot probes on the Moon.

Luna 16 was the first to land at night, eight days after taking off from the Earth. It managed to leave the surface again and came all the way back home carrying three and one-half ounces of rock samples from the Sea of Fertility.

Luna 17 arrived on November 17 and carried a roving vehicle which explored the Moon's surface.

Machina Speculatrix

Have you ever used a floor-turtle at school? It's a little robot that can be controlled from your classroom computer, and when its pen is down it draws pictures on a piece of paper (or right on the carpet if you forget the paper!).

FIRST APPEARANCE

A much earlier member of the robot-turtle family was shown at the Festival of Britain in 1950.

HOW DOES IT WORK?

The Machina Speculatrix, or Cybernetic Tortoise, as it was called, could move around on three wheels, avoiding obstacles and seeking out light. However, if the light was too bright it would back away.

CREATOR

Its inventor was Dr. William Grey. He was born in the United States, but studied in England, where he also invented the famous EEG brain topography machine.

VERSIONS

Dr. Grey actually made two of his robots, which he nicknamed Elsie and Elmer.

One of the original tortoises was rediscovered in 1995 and is now on display at the Science Museum in London.

Mahmud's Robots

Over seven hundred years ago, the Sultan Mahmud had little mechanical men who could pour liquid into his royal goblet.

AUTOMATIC HAND DRYER

He also had robotic peacocks that filled his washbasin with fresh water, followed by little metal servants with perfumed talc and towels to dry and powder his hands. These marvels were some of the first-ever mechanical servants, whose only purpose was to please their master — indeed, the sign of a good robot!

Maria

Mean, metal, and magnificent — that's Maria! She is one of the all-time classic robots of movie history and star of the 1920s film *Metropolis*.

AUTHOR

Thea Von Harbou wrote the film script, then later the book. The setting is Metropolis, a city of the future.

CREATOR

Maria was created by a mad scientist called Rotwang. He lives near Metropolis where the rich enjoy every pleasure, while the poor workers are slaves, operating huge machines underground. Rotwang, who's upset about losing his beloved sweetheart Hel, re-creates her as a robot, then transforms his robot into the form of Maria, one of the citizens of Metropolis, with disastrous consequences. The robot Maria is evil and the workers chase after her and destroy her by fire.

MOVIE CLASSIC

The original German film of 1926 was directed by Fritz Lang, who just happened to be Thea Von Harbou's husband. It was made in black and white and was a silent movie with fancy piano playing for special effects. It quickly became a classic.

FAMOUS SCENE

In the famous robot scene, Maria looked amazing. She was sleek and metallic — quite eerie. She sat in a chair behind a curtain and was unveiled by her creator, Rotwang.

"All it is missing is a soul," he uttered.

The whole plot had a pretty grim view of the future. Good thing it didn't turn out that way!

Marvel-Men Robots

The Marvel comic books of the 1960s included dozens of superheroes and their enemies. Among them were robots and cyborgs with special powers and deadly weapons.

BORIS-BOT

One of bad guys was Titanium Man — also known as Boris the Merciless. He wore a robotic suit that helped him to fly and fire lasers. None of this was enough to help him defeat the great Iron Man, however.

SENTINELS

The Marvel X-Men comics feature the Sentinels, who fight the X-Men with blaster rays built into their wrists. They have special equipment that helps them to work out the best way of defeating their opponents.

LEADER

The X-Men are humans with special powers, led by Xavier at his Institute for Higher Learning in New York.

WOLVERINE

The cyborg-hero called Logan (code name Wolverine) has indestructible metal parts attached to his skeleton. Long metal claws shoot out from his hands and take the enemy by surprise. Wolverine's skin has the ability to heal itself immediately, so his claws never cause him any harm. With his deadly samurai fighting skills, he is a very useful member of the team.

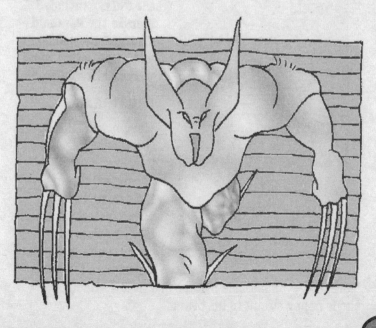

SPACEKNIGHTS

Another band of Marvel comic-book robots are the Cyborg Spaceknights, an army of aliens led by Rom. They practice dark magic and travel the universe trying to conquer other planets, including the Earth. The Spaceknights are really a breed of aliens called Dire Wraiths, with technology such as an armored robot, Watchwraith, one of their deadliest weapons.

Marvin the Paranoid Android

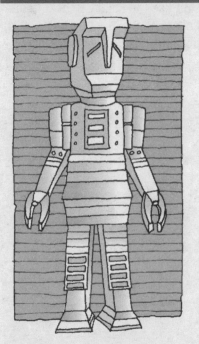

A famous radio and TV series called *The Hitchhiker's Guide to the Galaxy* included Marvin the Paranoid Android, the saddest and most boring robot in the entire universe.

CREATOR

Marvin was built by the Sirius Cybernetics Corporation and advertised throughout the galaxy as "Your plastic pal who's fun to be with." Fun, however, wasn't quite the right description for him. More like — "miserable metal contraption without a single happy circuit in his brain."

FATAL FLAW

His "Genuine People Personality Chip" was all too depressing for him or anyone else to cope with.

AUTHOR

The series was written by Douglas Adams, a young graduate of Cambridge University in England, who was spotted by Simon Brett of BBC Radio 4. The show first went on the air on March 8, 1978, with Stephen Moore as the voice of Marvin.

WHAT HAPPENED?

The Hitchhiker's Guide to the Galaxy, which also became a popular book, follows the exploits of Arthur Dent and his extraterrestrial pal, Ford Prefect, as they escape Earth just before an alien spaceship blows it up. The two of them travel the galaxy guided by an electronic book, which is said to be more popular than the best-seller *53 More Things To Do in Zero Gravity.*

Maximillian

There was once a Disney film called *The Black Hole,* about a black hole and the robots that went on a quest to investigate it. The biggest and baddest of them all was Maximillian or "Max II" for short.

SCIENCE FACT

Making a film about a black hole might seem rather pointless when you consider that nothing that gets anywhere near one stands a chance of surviving. The gravity of a black hole is so great that not even light can escape its pull. We're basically talking about a giant vacuum cleaner out in space that sucks up matter by the galaxy load.

MISSION

Max II is a big red robot on board the giant *Cygnus* spaceship. He was created by Dr. Reinhardt to help in his mad ambition to enter the black hole. Vincent and Bob are two good robots who meet up and do battle with him and his army of robot soldiers.

Mechagodzilla

Most of us shudder at the mention of Godzilla, the giant reptile that strikes fear into the hearts of sailors and Pacific islanders alike. But how many know of Mechagodzilla, the equally terrifying robot version?

SCREEN DEBUT

Mechagodzilla was the star of a 1974 film. The big, metal robot lizard rises up out of Mount Fuji and goes on a rampage in downtown Tokyo. Its alien creators hadn't bet on meeting the real Godzilla, however, who swiftly comes to the rescue along with a giant fluffy dog monster called King Seeser. There's also a spy called Namara and Professor Miyajima, the one with all the brains.

Metal Mickey

A British television show from the early 1980s featured a tubby little robot with a sense of humor. His name was Metal Mickey.

FAMILY FAVORITE

Metal Mickey lived with a real-live family including Mom (Stringbean), Dad, and their kids Haley, Steve, and Janey. Mickey was quite partial to atomic thunderbusters, which always kept him happy.

FAMOUS PHRASES

Metal Mickey was likely to say all sorts of ridiculous things and utter phrases such as "Boogie, Boogie" and how about:

Ready, steady are you set,

For Metal Mickey,

He's the greatest robot yet.

He's Metal Mickey!

CREATOR

The show was produced by one of the zany 1960s Monkees pop stars, Mickey Dolenz, who shared Metal Mickey's name and did equally batty things himself.

Being able to fly like a dragonfly or a bat isn't an easy thing for a robot to do. But Microbat is an expert at it.

REQUIREMENTS

First of all, a robot has to be light enough to get airborne and its motor has to be powerful enough to flap a pair of wings.

CREATORS

Scientists at a spy-plane company called AeroVironment managed to build an eight-inch-long flapping robot called Microbat that can stay in the air for as long as its batteries will allow.

BATLIKE

They call it Microbat because it flaps its wings more like a bat than an insect, although they hope one day to be able to make a tiny robot that can hover slowly inside a building, avoiding walls and taking photographs as it goes — a real fly on the wall!

Tiny robots no bigger than a speck of dust are called microbots.

SCIENCE FACT

It may seem incredible, but scientists have already built microbots that can swim in salty water. They are made of silicon and gold and have tiny arms, wrists, and fingers.

WHAT CAN THEY DO?

In a tank at the Linkopings University in Sweden, a whole team of these microbots lifted up a glass bead as scientists controlled them with little pulses of electricity.

MICRO SURGERY

It's hoped that one day these tiny bots may be able to swim in the bloodstream, repairing damaged cells in human patients.

Mini-bot

No larger than a quarter-inch cube, the world's tiniest robot is powered by three watch batteries that allow its miniature computer brain to operate tracked wheels, two motors, and a temperature sensor.

CREATOR

This teeny-bot has been developed by the Sandia National Laboratory in New Mexico to crawl along pipes and perform tasks that larger robots are unable to do.

PERFORMANCE

It travels at the not-so-lightning speed of 20 inches per minute! That's 100 feet per hour, which means it would take over 52 hours to travel a mile.

RECORD BREAKER

In 2001, the Sandia robot was said to be the smallest mechanical robot in the whole world.

Muffy

In the film *Battlestar Galactica*, Muffy is a cute, pug-faced robot dog.

PURPOSE

It was built as a companion for Boxy, a young boy who stars in the film. Muffy can learn tricks just like a real dog and is programmed to bark and wag its tail, which is surprising when you realize that the robo-doggy itself was played by a chimpanzee in a costume!

My Real Baby

For the little girl who likes talking to her Barbies but never gets a reply, the toy company Hasbro has brought out "My Real Baby," which includes Natural Response Technology.

LIFELIKE

With 15 human emotions and realistic appearance, My Real Baby could almost pass for the genuine article. It looks and feels human and can move and respond in hundreds of different ways. Luckily, it has a handy little "sleep" button to keep the family happy when they've all had enough.

Nano-Technology

Imagine a robot so tiny that you could fit millions of them on the head of a pin. Now imagine that these robots can make other robots just like themselves and that they can move tiny atoms around one at a time. Impossible? Or is it?

TINY BUILDING BLOCKS

When Kim Eric Drexler was a young man he dreamt of just such robots. Back in 1992 he spoke to the U.S. government in Washington and told them about his ideas. He explained that it would soon be possible to take simple molecules like hydrogen, oxygen, and carbon and, using them as building blocks, make anything at all.

MEAT MACHINE

He described a machine that could take a handful of leaves and turn it into a piece of fresh beefsteak! All the machine would have to do was rearrange the molecules, putting them in just the same positions as they occur in a real piece of meat. Many people laughed and said it was impossible. No one could build such a machine. It was the stuff of films and fantasy — they said.

ALLIES

But others did take Drexler seriously. One famous scientist, Richard Feynman, who many thought to be as brilliant as Albert Einstein, had even come up with the idea himself 30 years earlier. He helped convince others that it wasn't as crazy as it seemed.

SCIENCE FACT

Already, scientists have found they can move individual molecules and even atoms themselves using a special microscope — the Scanning Tunneling Electron Microscope or STM.

HOW DOES IT WORK?

The STM was designed to "feel" its way across a surface instead of seeing it with light. The very tip of the microscope is a single atom wide and it is with this atom-tipped point that scientists can nudge and move other atoms around, one at a time.

TINY WRITING

Soon after learning this trick they could arrange atoms in all sorts of patterns. The IBM Corporation spelled out the letters IBM using just 35 atoms of xenon. It was so small that you had to measure it in nanometers — that's a billionth of a meter — less than one 39-billionth of an inch. Because of its incredibly small size, the technology of moving atoms and molecules around is now called nano-technology.

THINKING SMALL

Perhaps it's a good idea at this point to demonstrate how small an atom really is.

Imagine an earth-sized bag full of grapefruits. There would be as many grapefruits in that bag as there are atoms in a grain of sand. We're talking very, very small!

NANO-WALKERS

Now imagine some little three-legged bugs, running around like ants in a picnic basket. These little beauties may look like insects, but in fact they're robots — miniature nano-robots. They dance around on three legs, taking an incredible 4,000 steps per second. Each nano-walker is about an inch tall and has a probe like the tip of an STM microscope that can move molecules around.

CREATOR

They were invented by Sylvain Martel, and he says that thousands of them can be controlled using infrared radar, which will one day put them to work building nano-machines and quantum computers.

WHAT NEXT?

Nano-bots are the key that promises to unlock the door to newer and more incredible robots that can eat, regenerate themselves, and think like humans. Since Drexler and Feynman had their first dreams of nano-technology, we still haven't managed to gain total control over atoms and molecules. Scientists can move these little building blocks around, but they can't program nano-bots with the blueprints to make whatever they want, like a nice shiny new sports car. That's a very big challenge indeed.

ULTIMATE RECYCLING

When we do discover how to do that, then anything will be possible. You will then have a machine in your home that can make you the latest bike from a pile of rusty old nuts and bolts. You will be able to make presents for the whole family from all your old junk. The possibilities will be endless.

 # NEAR

On February 12, 2001, after a journey of many millions of miles, a little robot space probe gently touched down on the surface of the asteroid Eros. It was an amazing achievement.

LAUNCH

The NEAR Shoemaker craft set off back in 1996 and took exactly four years to reach its target, beginning a year-long orbit of the asteroid.

MISSION

NEAR discovered that Eros is a huge piece of cracked rock with large craters and massive boulders on its surface. It took over 160,000 photographs and could pick out details as small as one-third of an inch in size.

 # NeCoRo

NeCoRo means Robot Cat in Japanese, and it's a gray-and-brown fluffy mechanical feline.

WHAT CAN IT DO?

This techno-puss sits on its owner's knee and can purr, twitch, and make 48 different kinds of noises, depending on how it is treated. With a battery life of only one and a half hours it's also really good at sleeping!

CREATORS

The cat's maker, Omron, hasn't given it the ability to run away and catch mice, so there's no chance that your robo-pet will ever get stuck up a tree!

 # Ninja

Imagine being able to climb up walls using suction cups on the ends of your legs! Well, there's a fantastic Spider-Man-style robot that can do exactly that.

FUNCTION

Ninja was designed to carry out inspection and repair work on bridges and buildings. The first prototype was built in 1990, with an improved model, Ninja 2, developed in 1994.

PERFORMANCE

It may not be fast at 25 feet per minute, but it's a lot easier than using tons of scaffolding to get the job done.

 # Nomad

Roaming across the vast Antarctic ice fields, a shiny four-wheeled robot had a job to do back in February 2000. It was called Nomad and it was looking for meteorites.

CREATOR

The Robotics Institute of Carnegie-Mellon University, Pittsburgh.

MISSION

Nomad led the expedition that identified five meteorites from outer space that had landed in the icy snows of Elephant Moraine near the South Pole. This expedition is paving the way for future polar expeditions and missions to the Moon and Mars.

RECORD BREAKER

In July 2001 Nomad set a world record for being the robot to travel the farthest on its own, trekking 133 miles across the rugged Atacama Desert in Chile. Nomad roamed around collecting meteorites and fossils and took more than a million color photographs.

SPECIFICATIONS

It has four-wheel drive and runs at a top speed of just one mile per hour. Slow but sure!

ODV

The U.S. Navy developed a robotic vehicle in the early 1980s based on a wheel that could move in different directions — the Omni Directional Vehicle.

WHAT CAN IT DO?

It is a simple beast, but is good at moving missiles, spare parts, engines, and other heavy objects on board ships. Because a ship may be rocking violently in the waves, ODVs must be very steady and reliable.

Patches

The Randleman, North Carolina, Fire Department has a great little robot teacher — a Dalmatian pup called Patches, built by Robotronics.

WHAT CAN IT DO?

Patches sits at the wheel of his fire truck, Pumper, and warns schoolchildren all about the dangers of fire.

OTHER VERSIONS

These include Pluggie, the robot fire hydrant, who speaks to thousands of children each year in schools and scout groups in North Carolina. There's Freddie the Fire Truck who moves, speaks, and sounds his siren — all by remote control. He can wink, blink, and move his eyes, too. There are two fire dogs called Sparky and Freckles, and, of course, Buzz E. Detector and his House of Hazards.

Who knows how many lives are saved by instructor-bots like these?

On Independence Day in 1997, a plummeting robot craft tore through the thin Martian atmosphere and prepared for final descent. It was the *Pathfinder* probe and it carried on board a little six-wheeled rover called *Sojourner*.

BOUNCE-DOWN!

A huge parachute opened up, followed by enormous inflatable air bags. Moments later the lander hit the rocky surface of Mars. It bounced 50 feet back up again, then fell down under a gravitational pull a third that of the Earth. The craft bounced a further fourteen times like a huge rubber beach ball, finally coming to rest as the bags deflated.

MARTIAN ROVER

Two days later, *Pathfinder* got the mission under way as its little six-wheeled rover vehicle, *Sojourner*, rolled down from the lander and began its exploration of the planet's surface. *Pathfinder* had a few problems finding the right path for *Sojourner*, but eventually the Mars buggy set off and roamed around like a remote-controlled toy on a mission.

TIME DELAY

It takes ten minutes for signals to get from Earth to Mars, so *Sojourner* wasn't all that quick. After nearly three months of exploring and careful experiments, the probe lost contact with Earth and fell silent.

FUTURE MISSIONS

Many more robot expeditions to Mars are planned over the next few years, to check for water and prepare landing sites for a mission with humans aboard. One day we will see robots beginning construction of a permanent base on the red planet. Today there are hundreds of research scientists and astronauts preparing for the time when people can live on Mars. The ISS (International Space Station) is being built early this century for scientific research. Many experiments will be carried out there on adapting the human body for life in space. Up until now there have been serious difficulties arising from life in the weightless environment of space. Bones disintegrate and the heart becomes weak.

All of this has to be sorted out before humans can risk voyages to the planets lasting several months. And when they do go to Mars, NASA's latest robots will be going along for the ride.

Pino

Pino has a long, pointy nose, but he isn't made of wood, and his ears are bright green and made of plastic.

CREATOR

Named after the puppet Pinocchio, Pino was built by Hiroaki Kitano at the Japanese firm ZMP in 1999, making his official appearance on April 18 of the following year.

SPECIFICATIONS

He stands 29 inches tall and weighs in at 18 pounds. He is covered in 35 separate plastic panels, which cover 150 moving mechanical parts. A total of 29 motors operate different movements such as walking and turning.

CYBER-STAR

Pino walks and dances and has so far starred in a pop video, "Can You Keep a Secret?" with Japanese singer Hikaru Utada. The company hopes to develop and program its creation as a home-help robot.

ROBOT REALITY | **Pod** | TECHNO TOY

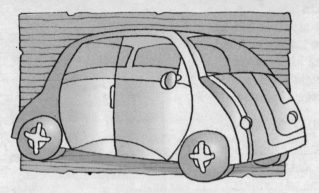

Is it a car, or is it a robot? Pod is both.

FEATURES

Push the button on your mini-controller and the doors of the Pod concept car slide apart. Its lights blink yellow to show it's happy to see you, and as you climb aboard, your favorite music starts to play inside the vehicle.

CREATORS

Built by the Toyota Car Company together with Sony, it is both a means of transportation and a state-of-the-art hi-fi system.

PROTOTYPE

The first prototype was shown at the 2001 Tokyo Motor Show.

HOW DOES IT WORK?

From the outside it may look like a regular car, but the inside is very different. There's no steering wheel, accelerator, or brake pedal. The driver uses a finger pad to operate all the controls instead. James Bond would be impressed! Mention the name of any singer or band while you're driving and Pod will find their music on the Internet, download it, and turn up the volume.

Quantum Computer

Modern robots need computer circuits the way we humans need brains. They can't operate without them, and the future of superfast robot brains lies in the technology of quantum computing.

SHRINKING COMPUTERS

If you had wanted to own a computer back in 1970 you would have needed to give it your whole bedroom. Ten years later, a computer with similar capabilities could fit on your tabletop. At the beginning of the twenty-first century you can own a computer with much more power than the ones that landed men on the Moon and it need be no larger than the size of a paperback book.

At this rate, we'll soon be walking around with incredible computer capability built into wristwatches, hearing aids, and the ring on your little finger.

ATOMIC LEVEL

Back in the early 1980s, a researcher called Richard Feynman began to think about a new kind of technology. It is known as quantum computing. Feynman realized that, unlike the electrical microchips of the time, computers could be much, much smaller — as small as a few atoms across.

HOW DO THEY WORK?

At such a tiny scale things work very differently than they do in the world that we see. Crazy though it might seem, in the quantum world, tiny electronic switches can be both on *and* off at the same time! This leads to much faster processing times, and possibilities that were previously unthinkable.

NEURAL NETWORKS

The other advantage of these brains is the possibility for "neural networking." This means that artificial brains can grow and expand, constantly making new connections just as a human brain can. This is pretty much what Arthur C. Clarke had in mind when he wrote about the HAL–9000 computer in his space odyssey story (see page 62).

 R100

It looks like a Russian doll on wheels, but there isn't a nest of smaller robots inside!

CREATOR

The R100 is a prototype personal help robot developed by the NEC Central Research Lab.

WHAT CAN IT DO?

It can recognize your face, talk to you, obey commands, and find its way around the home. Video camera eyes and directional ears mean it can find you wherever you are in the house, and tell you when new e-mail has arrived on your computer.

R2-D2

The film director George Lucas wrote a great fantasy story and made it into a science-fiction movie back in 1977. It was called *Star Wars* and it featured one of the most popular robots of all time: R2-D2.

MISSION

This little fellow and C-3PO are best friends (when they're not arguing) and they help Luke Skywalker and Princess Leia to fight the evil Empire.

SPECIAL FEATURES

Artoo-Detoo (R2-D2) is designed to help pilots in deep space. He has a great collection of tools and gadgets such as a radar eye, 3-D holographic film projector, electric shock prod, fire extinguisher, power saws, periscope, and a grasping claw. He gets around on two tracked legs with an extra leg for support when he needs it.

Robby, the Robot

And now for some real sci-fi — a full-color spectacular movie: *The Forbidden Planet*, starring Robby, the Robot.

ORIGIN

The film was based on the play *The Tempest* by William Shakespeare — only it featured a marvel of a mechanical man-servant called Robby.

SPECIFICATIONS

He is just what the imagination conjures up when the word "robot" is used ... big and black, with a transparent cone-shaped head. Dials and lights whizzed and whirled about in glorious Technicolor, and the audience loved it.

CREATOR

Robby was the invention of Robert Kinoshita, who also designed the B9 robot for *Lost in Space* in the 1960s. Robby cost $125,000 to build.

OPERATOR

He was originally operated by the actor, Frankie Darrow, and could walk, talk, and rescue damsels in distress.

WELCOMING PARTY

As the crew of the United Planets Cruiser C-57D lands on the planet Altair IV, Robby comes to greet them, zooming up in a cloud of dust across the desert. He takes them to his maker, the mysterious Dr. Morbius.

WHAT HAPPENED?

Strange things happen on the planet and the crew members barely escape with their lives as an evil invisible monster, the Id, tries to kill them. In the final scene, Robby takes control of the space cruiser and safely steers a course for Earth.

OTHER APPEARANCES

Robby later starred in *The Invisible Boy*, *The Addams Family*, *Mork and Mindy*, and numerous commercials.

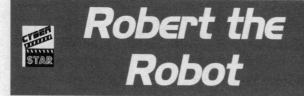

Robert the Robot

Starring in 39 episodes of the 1960s puppet production *Fireball XL5*, Robert the Robot was a member of the World Space Patrol.

SETTING

Set in the year 2067, the series is full of futuristic technology. Robert the Robot joins Steve Zodiac and the crew of *Fireball XL5* patrolling Sector 25.

ENEMIES

Robert helps to seek out villains such as the Green Men, the Subterraneans, and Mr. & Mrs. Space Spy.

Robin 4DOF

Being able to crawl along bridges, airplane wings, ships, and buildings checking for faults and weaknesses, is a difficult job for humans, but not for Robin (ROBotic INspector) 4DOF

HOW DOES IT WORK?

Robin can walk along any surface using four rubber suction cups.
It has a long umbilical cord linking it to a master computer.

CREATOR

Robin 4DOF was invented in 1996 by Robert Pack at Vanderbilt University.

Robocop

It would be a good idea to throw down those weapons and do as this cyber star says.

ORIGIN

In the movie *Robocop*, after police officer Alex Murphy is shot dead, his central nervous system is combined with a nearly indestructible cyborg body and he becomes Robocop, the toughest cop on the beat, and the answer to Old Detroit's rampant crime.

CREATOR

Developed by Omni Consumer Products, Inc. (OCP).

FAMOUS PHRASES

"Think it over, creeps!"

"Dead or alive . . . you're coming with me!"

TELEVISION VERSIONS

In 1997 work began on turning *Robocop* into an animated television series, with 40 half-hour episodes. Then in 2001 came a mini series — *Robocop Prime Directive* with live-action crime fighting against a new enemy — a high-tech terrorist called Albert Bixler, a.k.a. Bone Machine. Murphy's directives are pretty straightforward:

- Serve the public trust
- Protect the innocent
- Uphold the law

TECHNO TOY *RoboCup*

In the early 1990s, researchers in Japan came up with the idea of using the game of soccer as a great way of testing out their robots.

WHEN DID IT ALL KICK OFF?

By 1996 the rules had been drawn up and experimental matches were being played. In 1997 the first RoboCup games were held at the Artificial Intelligence Conference in Nagoya, Japan, with roaring success. Over 40 teams participated, with over 5,000 spectators cheering them on.

HUMANOID LEAGUE

In the Fukuoka, Japan, games in 2002, a new humanoid robot league began, including some great two-legged players. Other leagues include:

Simulation League

Small Robot League

Full-Set Small Robot League, with 11 robots per team

Middle-Size Robot League

Sony Legged Robot League

 Robodoc

Everyone likes to trust a doctor. They're smart and highly trained, and we put our lives in their hands. So how much trust would you have if the doctor about to whip out your tonsils happened to be a robot? Well, here are some reasons why Robo-doctors should be given a chance.

STEADY HANDS

Part of the challenge of being a top surgeon is accuracy. You have to be able to cut with your scalpel in just the right place, to just the right depth. Mistakes could be disastrous.

With robot surgeons in the operating theater you stand a much better chance. Robots can measure things perfectly and they have very steady hands.

FIRST PATIENT

By 1990, robots could perform routine surgery in a fraction of the time that humans had been able to. In June of that year a mechanical surgeon called Robodoc carried out the first-ever operation on a live patient. The patient was a cute little dog with an injured leg and some very careful bone surgery was needed to replace a hip joint.

OPEN-HEART HELPER

Soon, robots were being used to assist doctors in heart and general surgery. Dr. Damiano at the Hershey Medical Center was one of the first to use robots. His robots would hold open parts of the heart during operations. They could also operate cameras and move instruments with amazing precision — a wobble factor of less than a millionth of an inch. Robot cameras can magnify the area being operated on and do exactly as they are told, without ever losing their concentration.

VERSIONS

Machines such as AESOP, ZEUS, and HERMES were some of the first Robo-doctors. They each had an arm that had been developed by NASA for space missions. By the middle of the twenty-first century there will be many robotic aids for doctors, able to assist regularly with routine operations.

REMOTE CONTROL

In September 2001, surgeons in New York managed to perform a remotely controlled operation on a patient in Strasbourg, France, over 3,800 miles away. The 68-year-old woman had her gall bladder removed by a three-armed robot called ZEUS. Doctors are looking into all sorts of ways in which they can use this same kind of tele-robotic surgery — perhaps in disaster areas, or on battlefields, where it is difficult for doctors to go.

SPACE "PROBE"

NASA has developed a robotic probe that can enter a person's brain and find cancerous tumors. It learns quickly which is good brain tissue and which is bad, slowly making its way to the problem spot. It can even detect blood vessels and avoid damaging them on its journey. So what does NASA have to do with surgery, you ask? Well, on long space journeys they hope one day to send robot doctors along with the crew for emergency operations in space.

Robo-Dozer

Putting buildings on Mars will be necessary when astronauts finally get there. And that means they'll need machines to do all the hard work.

MINIATURE HEROES

Sending full-size bulldozers to Mars would be out of the question. But tiny ones weighing about eight pounds have been devised by NASA to scoop up the Martian soil and dump it elsewhere.

TEAMWORK

Whole teams of mini robotic bulldozers could be operated from a central control tower. They have arms to dig and turn themselves the right way up if they topple over. Above their arms are buckets to carry soil and rubble away from the excavation site.

Robo-Fish

It may be the most realistic robot in the world . . . a robotic fish that swims like the real thing, but is in fact a battery-operated muscle.

BACKGROUND

Scientists have been able to control real muscles using electricity since Luigi Galvani's experiments with frogs' legs in 1786. Two hundred years later, Hugh Herr at the Massachusetts Institute of Biomechatronics put real muscles into a robot fish he was building and had it swimming around in a tank of sugar water. (The sugar was used to give the frog muscles the energy they needed.)

FUTURE PLANS

Eventually he wants to use the same idea to operate artificial arms and legs for humans. He has a good reason for doing this — Herr lost his own legs after they became frostbitten and had to be amputated below the knee.

OTHER VERSIONS

A robot tuna and pike have also been spawned to test fishlike movement underwater. Researchers watched real fish to see exactly how they swim.

Pelicans are fascinating to watch at the zoo, but when they start eating all the fish in your pond, something has to be done. Sounds like a job for Robo-Gator!

CREATORS

In the Florida Everglades, officials called in researchers from Louisiana State University to help them deal with their own pelican problem. The result was a floating scarecrow shaped like an alligator with paddles and a bird-spotting camera.

HOW DOES IT WORK?

Once the robot spots a pelican it shoots out a powerful jet of water to scare it away. Sensors keep the pelican-scarer from bumping into banks and make sure that it patrols the whole lake evenly.

Robo-Pharaoh

Yes, even the ancient Egyptians had to get in on the act. They carved stone gods and made masks that came alive with moving, talking mouths.

HOW DID THEY WORK?

Hidden operators would talk through tubes leading to their mouths, giving the impression that the statues and figures were alive and could speak. It was exactly the same way that the old professor tricked Dorothy and her friends by pretending to be the Wizard of Oz in the famous film.

MUMMY'S DAY PRESENTS

The Egyptians also had wooden dolls of beasts and gods with movable arms that they buried in their great tombs and pyramids. There were some with the heads of lions, birds, and jackals. Some had simple hinged arms that could be moved. Perhaps they were designed to come alive and help the pharaoh in his next life — royal robotic assistants.

Robot Ears

Ears for robots come in the form of ultrasonic sensors. Microphones and detectors can pick up noises that are too faint, too high, or too low for humans to hear.

SUPER-SENSITIVE

Robots can detect footsteps and pins being dropped at a distance. Imagine if instead of using that grumpy

Doberman as a guard-dog, you could have Doberbot, the security guard dog that can hear a hamster cleaning its paws three blocks away?

Robot Wars

Robot Wars involves menacing-looking robots in a battle to the death, a face-off that takes place in a dark and scary stadium with flames, obstacles, and crash barriers.

DO IT YOURSELF

Viewers were soon inspired to dash off to their garages and garden sheds to build a whole host of radio-controlled do-it-yourself robots to enter into the competition.

ORIGINS

Robot Wars was an idea that started back in 1992. A young amateur robot builder called Marc Thorpe decided to add remote control to his mom's vacuum cleaner. Opening up his toolbox on the kitchen table, he took the cleaner apart and rebuilt it as a mean fighting machine — a vacuum cleaner with an attitude!

EARLY COMPETITIONS

Two years later, Marc created *Robot Wars*. Over a thousand people crowded into the Fort Mason Center in San Francisco, California, and watched as a few hopeful roboteers battled it out to the death. Wheels, wires, and wheelchair motors were scattered everywhere and the competition was a huge success. By 1996 there were 75 battling robots taking part.

HALL OF FAME

Some of the top Robot Warriors are Chaos 2; Hypno Disc, with its psychedelic disc spinning at 750 revs per minute; Razer, sporting its ten-ton hydraulic piercer, and Panic Attack II, which has dazzling yellow-and-black body armor, is powered by two truck windscreen wiper motors, and has lethal lifting forks as its secret weapon. The official house robots, made to muster up mayhem for competitors, include Sir Killalot, Sergeant Bash, and of course the dinosaur of destruction herself — Matilda.

FUTURE WARS

In years to come there may be humanoid and android warriors battling it out like gladiators on our 3-D screens every night. Now *there's* a thought.

Robosaurus

If the robots in this book so far are not mean enough for you, then meet Robosaurus.

SPECIFICATION

He's a 42-foot-high CARnivorous robot (twice as tall, and three times as heavy as a T rex) that breathes fire and eats cars for breakfast. Robosaurus uses foot-long steel teeth to rip their roofs off in a single bite.

CREATOR

Monster Robots Inc.

COST

$2.2 million.

GUEST APPEARANCES

Robosaurus performs at exhibitions around the world, and even invites someone in the audience to ride in its head. It has also starred in at least three films.

HOW DOES IT WORK?

It has massive gripping claws that pick up real cars and planes, and twistable wrists so it can drink from 30-gallon oil drums. The operator straps himself into a seat in Robo's head and controls its arms with his own arm movements. Foot pedals allow him to drive forward and steer left or right.

Rock 'em Sock 'em Robots

TECHNO TOY

Long before Lennox Lewis or Mike Tyson were packing punches, there were "Rock 'em Sock 'em Robots."

CREATOR

The game was made by the toy company Marx in 1966, and didn't even require batteries to make it work — just hand-operated controller arms on either side of the ring.

CONTENDERS

In the red corner we had the Red Rocker, and in the blue corner, Blue Bomber. Kids back in the 1960s battled their bots in a special boxing ring, trying to get their robots to punch their opponents in the jaw. If the spring-loaded head of your opponent's robot flew up out of its shoulders, you won!

MOVIE SHOWING

The battling duo made a guest appearance in *Toy Story II*.

Rosie the Robot

This helpful cartoon character scooted around our TV screens in the 1960s, dusting off the cobwebs and making cups of tea.

DOMESTI-BOT

She was the obedient little busybody who took care of all the housework for George and Jane Jetson in their futuristic cartoon series. Rosie, in her neat little pinafore would scurry around with a duster in the Jetsons' Skypad apartment block. It was a space-age version of the popular *Flintstones* cartoon, made by the same animators, Hanna-Barbera.

Elroy and Judy were the Jetson kids who were joined by Astro, their space-age hound.

ROBOT REALITY — *Rover*

You've heard of Babe the sheep-pig. Now there's Rover the sheep-bot. It's a techno solution to the problem of rounding up flocks of animals.

CREATORS

The Robot Sheepdog Project (RSP) was a joint effort of three British universities.

FARMYARD TRIALS

Instead of sheep, the researchers decided to test their robot out on ducks. Experiments with real live ducks were successful and the feathered fowl were neatly rounded up and taken to their pen.

SPECIFICATIONS

Rover is a cylinder on wheels and is designed to work outdoors on short grass. It is 11 inches tall and 17 inches wide with a soft plastic cover. Rover is mounted on rubber springs to make sure the ducks don't get hurt.

TOP SPEED

It can zoom along up to 9 mph, easily out-waddling the ducks.

HOW DOES IT WORK?

There is the robot vehicle, a computer, and a camera. Information from the camera helps the computer to decide a path for rounding up the ducks. Commands are then sent by radio to the robot, which guides them to their pen.

TECHNO TOY — RS-01 Robot Dog

Twice the size of Aibo, the RS-01 is set to rival its Japanese counterpart with all-new tricks and features.

CREATOR

It has been developed by Nick Wirth and his team at the U.K. company RoboScience.

FUNCTIONS

The RS-01 will be able to recognize its owner's voice and even read out e-mail messages. Perhaps it can even fetch the morning newspaper!

 BOOK Bot — R.U.R.

The first-ever work of fiction to include the word robot was a play. It was written by a storyteller in Czechoslovakia, Karel Capek.

NEW WORD

Karel had just turned 30 when he sat at his desk to create what would be his most famous work ever — *R.U.R.*

(*Rossum's Universal Robots*). He would go down in history as the man who gave the word "robot" to the English language.

WHAT HAPPENED?

In the story, a brilliant scientist called Rossum lives with his son on a remote island where they create humanoid workers in a factory. The robots are made in huge, bubbling vats and mechanical looms spin miles of veins to carry blood through their artificial bodies.

FATAL FLAW

The one thing the robots lack is a soul. They are built to work — efficiently and cheaply. Rossum's coldhearted son discarded everything not needed for their mundane purpose. As the story progresses, a humanitarian aid worker, Helena Glory, persuades the factory director to give the robots a soul.

MEGA-MISTAKE

Oops! That's when it all goes horribly wrong. Instead of becoming kind, lovable robots, they wage war with humans and kill all of them. (It would be many years before Isaac Asimov would invent his fictional three rules for human and robot safety — see page 67.)

FATE OF THE BROTHERS

The story of Karel and his brother Josef was just as tragic. Karel was due to be arrested by Hitler's gestapo at the start of World War II. He died from pneumonia in 1938 before they could get to him. His brother Josef perished in a Nazi concentration camp at the end of the war.

Scallop

ROBOT REALITY

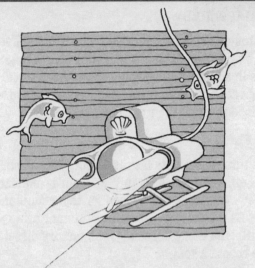

There really isn't anywhere on Earth or in space that robots can't go. Here's one that carries out a range of tasks underwater.

HOW DOES IT WORK?

This one-eyed robotic submarine with powerful search lights dives down beneath the waves. It is propelled by three variable-speed thruster motors and gets busy, often in cold waters and places where it's too dark and hazardous for human divers.

OTHER VERSIONS

A similar robot submersible, *Jason Junior,* was sent down to inspect the wreck of the *Titanic,* which famously sank in the North Atlantic in 1912. Others, such as *Scorpio II* and *Deep Drone,* can operate thousands of feet below the surface, mapping out the oceans or investigating sunken vessels.

Scorpion

Built for desert survival, but without a sting in its tail.

MISSION

Solving problems is an important part of robot design. A group of scientists in Boston have designed Scorpion, a 19-inch-long robot, which is set to travel across the Mojave Desert in California. It will have to clamber over rough terrain, find a target, and return — a total distance of almost 50 miles. Scorpion will have to survive in extreme conditions and overcome all sorts of obstacles.

CREATORS

Scientists at Northeastern University in Boston have studied real live scorpions to see how they behave and hope to be able to use robots like this to carry out spy missions for the military.

Slugbot

Forget the salt or package of slug pellets. What you need to protect your prize lettuces is a Slugbot.

CREATORS

Researchers at the University of West England have designed this robot that eats slugs and turns them into fuel for its onboard motor. It's an example of what scientists call a gastrobot (see page 57).

TECHNO TOY Soccer-bots

Playing soccer on a table with small robotic vehicles as players is a popular pastime for some people.

TABLETOP TECHNOLOGY

Specially designed robots have to push and bump the ball around, maneuvering carefully to score goals. It's a difficult game, and the robots have to be quite sophisticated, which means you won't find many of your pals playing this on the kitchen table. See also *RoboCup* (page 110) for full-sized robotic soccer.

ROBOT REALITY Spy-Cye

This helpful piece of hardware can roam around your home or office checking that the pizza hasn't burned to a crisp or the boss hasn't fallen asleep at her computer terminal.

CREATOR

"Probotics."

HOW DOES IT WORK?

The Spy-Cye is a personal robot, about 16 inches wide, that's controlled from your own PC using special software. Wherever you drag the computer mouse, Spy-Cye will follow. Armed with a built-in video camera, it will check on whatever you want to see but can't get to personally.

ONLINE

This robot's real usefulness is revealed when you realize that by connecting to your Spy-Cye via the Internet you can be in a different country and still see what's going on back home. So, the next time your family jets off on vacation to the Caribbean, leave Spy-Cye in charge of your precious jewels.

CYBER-SCHEDULE

It can be programmed to visit certain places at exact times using a computer diary, and will find its own way back to the battery charger when it runs out of power.

Star Wars Droids

Besides the legendary C-3PO and R2-D2 there are all sorts of other interesting robots that feature in the *Star Wars* films. Here are a few of them.

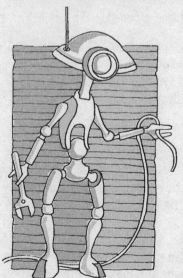

DUM-4 PIT DROIDS

When it comes to fixing Pod Racers and other vehicles, the DUM–4s are handy little robots to have around. They can use ordinary tools, and carry spare parts to get you back on the road in no time.

BATTLE DROIDS

Carried into battle in large MTT transport vehicles, the Federation's front-line robots quickly unfold and form ranks of formidable fighting machines. They can also ride on floating gun platforms called STAPs (Single Trooper Aerial Platforms) or drive Battle Tanks in teams of four. In the film *Episode I — The Phantom Menace,* Battle Droids are foiled in a skirmish against the Gungan Army when their control ship is destroyed out in space.

OOM-9 COMMAND BATTLE DROID

It looks like an ordinary foot droid, but is much more intelligent and leads entire armies into battle.

PROBE DROID

Zooming across open territory or lurking behind walls and buildings, the probe droid is a fully armed robot spy. It is equipped with a large camera eye and can track down its target wherever it may be hiding.

TC-3 PROTOCOL DROID

It looks like C-3PO, but comes in a variety of colors and finishes. Unlike C-3PO, who is especially intelligent for a protocol droid, TC-3s usually have their memories erased and are kept as simple servants and butlers.

GNK POWER DROID

When it's extra battery life you need, call one of these. It looks like a picnic box on legs, and makes a funny gonking noise.

WORKER DROID

When it comes to heavy lifting jobs, DUM-4s are hopeless. Worker droids like Otoga 222s and Rolos perform this kind of work.

DESTROYER DROID

A robot on three legs with fierce firepower. This droid transforms from the speedy P-59 wheel droid on command.

DROID STARFIGHTER

This battling spaceship is equally at home out in space or down on a planet's surface. Like all Federation droids, Starfighters are controlled by a giant mother ship.

On June 2, 1966, NASA landed its first *Surveyor* probe on the Moon and it had a very good reason for doing so.

TRAILBLAZER

Although very simple in design, this important pioneer paved the way for human Moon landings in 1969. It was followed by six other *Surveyor* robot probes, although two of these crashed and lost contact with Earth before they could complete their journeys.

MISSION

The main objective of the *Surveyor* landings was to take close-up photographs of the Moon's surface and decide if a manned landing would be safe. Each one had cameras attached and *Surveyors 3* and *7* carried soil scoops to pick up and test the lunar dust.

TECHNO TOY Tamagotchi

Back in 1997, if you hadn't heard of these little egg-shaped robo-pets you were seriously behind the times.

WHERE DID THEY COME FROM?

They hatched from tiny eggs after a cyberspace journey of millions of light years. With careful nurturing, a Tamagotchi would grow and eventually become a happy and contented creature, before returning to its home planet. Neglect it, and you'd have a grouch on your hands.

SELL-OUT

When they first appeared in Hong Kong, they all sold out within ten minutes. Soon the world had gone Tamagotchi-crazy and millions of homes had their own evolving cyber-pets bleeping and tweeting for attention.

Terminator

He's a T-800 robot sent back in time by a futuristic computer system called Skynet to change the course of history. And he promises to be back!

FILM HERO

Arnold Schwarzenegger, the famous bodybuilder and actor, played the part of the Terminator. He starred as the indestructible machine designed to eradicate humans who get in its way.

SILENT TYPE

Arnold utters only seventeen sentences during *Terminator I*.

ROBOT RIVAL

In the second film — *Terminator 2: Judgment Day*, Arnie had to fight a really cool shape-shifting robot called the T-1000. It could become liquid metal and turn into anything it liked. Terminator finally defeated the morphing man with a big pot of bubbling liquid metal.

TERMINATOR III

And the story doesn't end there. *Terminator III: Rise of The Machines* is underway.

Ten years after the second film is set, John Connor and the Terminator battle to protect themselves against an all-new female Terminator. Just like her cousins, she has incredible strength and abilities. Ms. Terminator has several new powers, too, like being able to disappear, morph herself into someone else, and even become pure energy.

BOOK Bot — *Tin Man* — CYBER STAR

WHAT HAPPENED?

Dorothy and her little dog, Toto, meet three friends on their way to see the Wizard of Oz in L. Frank Baum's children's story, which was first published in 1900. It later became one of the most popular films of all time, starring Judy Garland.

ROBOT WOODCUTTER

Along with a scarecrow and a lion, Dorothy follows the yellow brick road with the Tin Man, a mechanical woodcutter that hasn't got a heart. She finds him all rusted up and brings him back to life with a drop of good old engine oil.

OTHER SCREEN VERSIONS

In a 1964 TV version of the story in which Dorothy returns to the Land of Oz aboard a flying apple tree, Tin Man is given the name of Rusty. The 1985 film *Return to Oz* featured Tik-Tok, another mechanical man from the Oz books.

ROBOT REALITY

Tin Man II

Tin Man II isn't a man at all — it's a robotic wheelchair.

CREATOR

It was built by the KISS Institute for Practical Robotics (KIPR) in Oklahoma and can help those with serious disabilities to get around inside the home. Tin Man II can find its way through doors, follow hallways without bumping into walls, and make some decisions on its own.

NAMESAKE

The makers say it wasn't named after the metal man in *The Wizard of Oz*, but rather after a creature in episode 68 of the TV series *Star Trek: The Next Generation*.

OTHER VERSIONS

The institute has also built a robot chair called Wheelesley, which came first in a college wheelchair limbo contest to see how narrow a door the robot could guide itself through.

Tin-Plate Toy Robots

TECHNO TOY

Back in the 1950s, just about every toy box had at least one of these lurking somewhere down at the bottom. If you could find the key then all you had to do was wind 'em up and watch 'em go.

ACTION-PACKED

Tremendous Mike was one of dozens of tin-plate robots. He had real TURN-O-GO action with a sparkling screen and revolving radar on his head.

VARIETIES

Usually made in Japan, there were dozens to choose from, including Robby, the Robot, from the film *The Forbidden Planet;* Zoomer the Robot, waddling along wielding his tin-plate wrench; Chief Smoky with nonstop action, puffing out realistic smoke from his head; Jupiter Robot; Thunder Robot; and TV Robot.

Tobor the 8th Man

Tobor was a character in an old black-and-white Japanese cartoon from the 1960s. It was about Special Agent Brady who was killed and had his mind placed in a robot called 8th Man.

CREATOR

He is built by Professor Genius, whose son, Ken, is jealous and tries to defeat his father's creation.

ENEMIES

Besides the dreaded Ken, there were others for Tobor to outsmart, including Saucer Lips, Dr. Spectra, and the Butterfly Gang.

Transformers

Transformers ... robots in disguise!

CREATOR

"It is a world transformed, where things are not what they seem. . ."

That's what the company Hasbro said about its new toy back in 1984.

TOY INTO TOON

Originally little more than a collection of shape-shifting toy robots, the Transformers went on to become a classic cartoon series of the 1980s.

WHAT HAPPENED?

Their tale is a simple one: mechanical beings from the planet Cybertron are engaged in a civil war, with heroic Autobots dueling against the evil Decepticons. According to official Transformer history, the Autobots and Decepticons crashed into the Earth millions of years ago, were awakened in 1984 and continue to battle to this day. Here they made friends with humans such as Spike, Sparkplug, and Chip.

CHARACTERS

Kids soon became expert at twisting what to the untrained eye looked like a regular toy fighter plane into none other than the great "Starscream," or perhaps the beast machine Rhinox back into a four-footed African rhino. Five of the Autobots can even combine to make one colossal robot called Computron, which usually does battle with its archenemy Abominus.

FAMOUS PHRASES

Optimus Prime was famous for his battle cry, "We will put out the fires of evil!" and Super Ultra Magnus for, "Let's hit the road, Autobots!"

MOVIE VERSION

In 1986 the Transformers battled it out on the big screen and had a new robot enemy to contend with. Its name was Unicron and it could destroy anything in its path, including planets like Cybertron!

Tripods

Perhaps there never was a time when humankind didn't dream, tell stories, and write about robots. Homer (the Greek poet — not Bart's dad) did, and he was *really* ancient.

VULCAN'S HANDIWORK

The Greeks dreamed of imitating the gods and giving life to their creations. Even in their stories they invented human-made beings. The poet Homer wrote about them in his famous adventure *The Iliad,* which tells of mechanical golden servants crafted by Vulcan in his forge, and twenty robotic tripods riveted together and programmed to scurry around on golden wheels.

Tripods II

Back in the nineteenth century appeared a book called *The War of the Worlds* by H. G. Wells. Written in 1898, it tells of an alien invasion from Mars, and some terrifying robots called the Tripods.

WHAT HAPPENED?

Strange cylinders land on the Earth, close to London, and aliens emerge from them. They are huge, ugly, black creatures with tentacles and beaks. They have no digestive systems as they never eat — they steal the blood from other creatures and inject it straight into their own veins instead.

ROBOT MACHINES

The Martians attack earthlings in their robotic Tripod machines, which blast out heat rays and fire canisters of poisonous black smoke.

COUNTERATTACK

Here's how the first Tripod "gets it" from the good old British Army.

The shell burst clean in the face of the Thing. The hood bulged, flashed, was whirled off in a dozen tattered fragments of red flesh and glittering metal.

"Hit!" I shouted, with something between a scream and a cheer.

VICTORY

More Tripods are destroyed by the ironclad warship, the *Thunder Child*. Eventually all are defeated and the world is saved from destruction.

The book was an instant success and has become a great classic of literature. The original idea really belonged to H. G. Wells' older brother, Frank.

BROADCAST BLUNDER

In 1938, Orson Welles, a famous actor, read the *The War of the Worlds* as a play on CBS radio. All across the eastern United States people thought that the radio was transmitting a news broadcast and that the Martians really were invading Earth. They fled to the hills in panic, having to be reassured by the police that it was all just a story.

Tripods III

Based on a trilogy of books by John Christopher, *Tripods* was a BBC television series in the mid-1980s.

WHAT WERE THEY?

The Tripods were huge three-legged walking alien death machines that terrorized the country lanes of England, hunting for humans to blast or keep as slaves. Sounds rather familiar; didn't the Wells brothers come up with that idea?

SHORT RUN

After two seasons the show was cancelled — probably because the Tripods themselves rarely appeared in the episodes and viewers became rather disappointed.

 # Troody

Building a robot that can walk on two legs is a challenge for designers. One team at MIT (Massachusetts Institute of Technology) based their biped on a late cretaceous dinosaur called the Troodon.

WHAT CAN IT DO?

Standing 18 inches tall at the hips, Troody really can walk on her own, stepping out for up to half an hour at a time. After several years as a research robot, she was retired in June 2001, taking her place on the shelf along with "Spring Flamingo" and "Geekbot" — two more "also-rans."

 # *Twiki*

One of the future-pals of space traveler Buck Rogers is Twiki the robot. They both starred in the TV series *Buck Rogers in the Twenty-Fifth Century* in the early 1980s.

WHAT HAPPENED?

Captain William "Buck" Rogers is shot off into deep space after a tragic accident aboard his NASA spaceship in 1987. When the spacecraft returns to Earth, the year is 2491. Buck finds the planet in the aftermath of a nuclear war and is enlisted as a pilot in a space fighter squadron. Twiki becomes Buck's friend, as does Dr. Theopolis, a techno-brain that forms part of Earth's Computer Council.

CRICHTON

Twiki and Buck are also joined by Crichton, a robot built by the scientist Dr. Goodfellow in the second series. They all set off in the starship *Searcher* looking for Earth's lost people, who have fled into outer space.

SCREEN PERFORMERS

The actor who played Twiki was Felix Sill. His voice was provided by Mel Blanc, who was also responsible for many famous cartoon voices such as Bugs Bunny and Tweety Pie.

CREATOR

Buck Rogers first appeared in the 1930s as kids followed his adventures in comic strips, radio shows, and black-and-white films. With Wilma Deering and Dr. Huer, Buck fought against the evil Killer Kane and his super gangsters in the year 2440. In 1950, Buck Rogers made it onto TV screens when he woke up in a secret cave behind Niagara Falls.

Tyrannosaurus Rex-Bot

Never mind dusty old skeletons of dinosaurs. How about the real thing? Or at least a lifelike robotic replica.

REPTILE ROBOT

In 2001 the Natural History Museum in London unveiled a gigantic three-quarter-sized T rex to wow its visitors. Opening up its jaws with realistic movements, the 13-foot-high Robo-Rex even smells of rotting flesh and Jurassic swamps.

CREATOR

It was designed and built by Kokoro, a Japanese animatronics company. If you'd like to pick one up from the gift shop on the way out, it will cost you over $300,000 — leaving you short for a hamburger and the bus fare home! And at an incredible 23 feet in length it wouldn't fit very comfortably on your bedside cabinet.

TECHNO TOY Ullanta Robots

Imagine a team of wheely-bots scurrying around, dancing, acting out plays, and kicking footballs to each other.

WHO ARE THEY?

"Ullanta Performance Robotics" is a group that does exactly that. It was founded in 1995 in Waltham, Massachusetts, and is currently based in Los Angeles. Their motto is "Because everybody loves robots." The group is directed by Barry Werger, who developed his skills at the University of Southern California.

WHAT CAN THEY DO?

The "Pioneer 1" robots perform plays and show off their soccer skills to entertain amazed audiences around the world. Ullanta entered a team of five robots known as the "Spirit of Bolivia" in the world Robo-Soccer championships in Japan and came through victorious, without a single goal being scored against them.

WHAT'S IN A NAME?

The name Ullanta comes from an old Peruvian play called *Ollantay* that Barry plans to perform with his robots.

Unimate

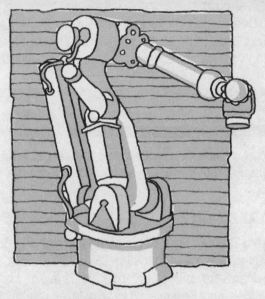

How would you like a job that's always exactly the same? Sounds boring, huh?

PERFECT WORKER

Imagine putting a thousand plastic door knobs into a thousand plastic bags every day for the rest of your life! A robot is much better suited because it never gets bored, doesn't need a coffee break, and can't make mistakes. It's the perfect assembly-line worker.

CREATOR

In 1959 the first such robot was sent to work for General Motors. It was called the Unimate and was designed by George C. Devol to unload parts from a machine to help build cars.

OTHER VERSIONS

Several other robot arms followed, including the Stanford arm, T3, the Vicarm, PUMA (Programmable Universal Manipulator for Assembly), and the Apprentice.

HOW DO THEY WORK?

Most of these worked by having a human operator put the arm through a set of movements to perform a certain task. After the robot arm had done the task once, it never forgot.

COMPUTER CONTROL

The first-ever robot arm to be completely controlled by a computer was the Cincinnati Milacron CH6, which started work in 1974. Modern computer-controlled arms don't need to be "taught" a particular job. They are smart enough to be programmed with plans of the finished product, which they then use to calculate their movements.

CYBER-SERVANTS

In 1978 the McDonnell-Douglas aircraft factory had enough robot assembly machines to cover 24 acres of factory floor space. All the worker robots were controlled by a master computer robot. Humans just checked that everything was in order and carried out routine maintenance. They were building some of the most sophisticated aircraft ever — with just a little help from human hands.

In the 1980s, smaller, cheaper robots were introduced, like the Tosman 200. Up to six of these amazing articulated arms would work together as a team, building and welding machines for companies like Nissan and Toshiba.

WHERE ARE THEY NOW?

Now robots operate in just about every engineering plant in the world. Car factories can produce hundreds of automobiles a day, and similar machines have been employed welding everything from ships and subs to tractors and trains.

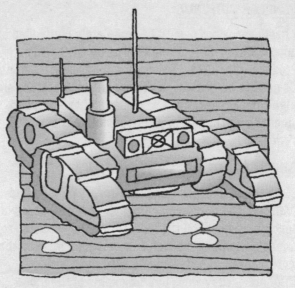

It can climb stairs and get around perfectly in urban environments.

WHAT CAN IT DO?

Urbie's main job is mobile military reconnaissance in city terrain, but many of its capabilities make it a useful assistant for police, emergency, and rescue services. The developers of Urbie hope to use him to investigate dangerous environments contaminated with radiation, biological weapons, or chemical spills. He could also be used for search-and-rescue in earthquake and disaster zones.

CREATORS

Urbie was developed as a team effort of JPL, iRobot Corporation, the University of Southern California, and Carnegie-Mellon University.

Vaucanson

In the mid-eighteenth century, a fantastic metal duck performed to packed audiences all over Europe. It was a show stealer and the work of Monsieur Jacques De Vaucanson.

SPECIFICATIONS

Each wing had over four hundred brass pieces, and its internal workings included a rubberized set of food pipes and intestines that allowed it to drink and eat just like the real thing.

DUCKY-DEMO

Expressions of disbelief on the faces of several members of the audience usually prompted a full demonstration of the duck's digestive abilities, which involved its gulping down little morsels of food and gurgling a glass or two of water.

OTHER CREATIONS

Not only did Jacques De Vaucanson create his duck, but he also designed and built some of the first life-sized android humans.

BELLRINGER-BOT

"The Bellringer" appeared at the festival of Germain in the 1750s. The stern-looking mechanical man held a bell in one hand and struck it rhythmically with a hammer. He was dressed in period costume and had wheels and moving parts concealed beneath his clothing.

PIGEON PERFORMANCE

There was also an elegant female android that performed gracefully along with a mechanical pigeon. She, too, was displayed at the festival, and when her clockwork mechanism was activated she lifted up her glass and had it filled with wine from the open beak of the pigeon perched with perfect balance on the top of her head. Just like the Bellringer, the lady and the pigeon were life-sized robots, with realistic features, clothing, and feathers.

EARLY EXPERIMENTS

Vaucanson started by making robotic angels while studying to be a Jesuit priest. They were probably hung from the oak beams of the local church and amazed and frightened congregations as they arrived for Mass on Sunday. The other priests didn't think much of his creations and smashed them all up.

Later he went on to build some really amazing mechanical people and animals. All of them were operated by clockwork with little gear wheels and strong metal springs inside. Some of them served food to guests and others played musical instruments.

MAGNUS THE MECHANIC

Monsieur Vaucanson wasn't the first builder of automata. Many had tried over the centuries with varying degrees of success.

Albertus Magnus was a thirteenth-century teacher who spent thirty years of his life building a mechanical man. It was rather stiff and clunky, but it could walk by itself and carried Albertus's books around for him. His every spare moment was devoted to the creature — improving and adjusting its intricate mechanical workings. But his student Thomas Aquinas thought that the mechanical servant was the work of the Devil and smashed it to bits. Albertus was horrified and is said to have cried out, "Thus perishes the work of thirty years." Thomas's grades probably went right down after a prank like that!

ROBOT REALITY **Viking**

The date was July 20, 1976 — the day that the Vikings invaded Mars!

WHAT HAPPENED?

This isn't the plot for a great new science fiction drama. It really did happen. After several failed attempts, NASA successfully landed the *Viking 1* space probe on the surface of Mars. Two months later they sent *Viking 2*.

MISSION

Falling from space at over 600 mph, the craft had to ignite its three main retro-rockets to slow itself down for a safe landing. Soon, the little machine with probes, cameras, and a robotic arm was busily scooping up samples of red rock and soil in the Chryse Planitia region of Mars. *Viking* had instruments for checking weather and atmosphere, and a sensor on one of its feet that acted as a temperature gauge. It was hoping to find life — perhaps some little bugs or bacteria.

WHAT DID IT FIND?

The results weren't very promising. *Viking* found nothing that looked remotely like an alien life-form. Eventually the batteries ran down on *Viking 1* and *2*, and they remain to this day on the dry surface of Mars — as dead as the soil they were sampling.

 VMS

Who would have thought of building a robot to milk cows? Probably some old farmer who was tired of having to get up at five o'clock each morning to do the job himself.

WHAT DOES IT STAND FOR?

Voluntary Milking System.

CREATORS

It is the work of a team from Silsoe Research Institute (SRI) in the U.K. and Alfa Laval Agri in Sweden.

HOW DOES IT WORK?

The robot has a vision-guided "soft" robot arm for attaching milking equipment. It can happily monitor and milk forty cows at a time all day long on the Hamra farm in Sweden. So you can turn off the alarm clock and roll over — leave it all to VMS.

Volto

This comical robot was featured in a black-and-white film made in 1941.

WHAT HAPPENED?

A gang of misfit kids make their way into Black's Department store and start looking around at the appliances. They meet Volto the robot. It's an exciting moment for all of them. Froggy, Spanky, Darla, and the rest of the kids were "Our Gang," later known as "The Little Rascals," and the film goes on to show them attempting to build a robot of their own.

MOW-BOT

In one scene, the neighborhood bully cunningly tries to sell the gang a box full of "invisible rays" for their robot. Later on, one of the gang climbs inside the robot suit and runs wild with a lawn mower, destroying flower beds in his wake. It raised plenty of laughs back then.

Voyager

Not all robotic space probes have made actual landings on the planets. Some have been launched solely to wander through the solar system, filming and photographing our nearest neighbors from close orbit.

SPACE ODYSSEY

Voyager craft performed the earliest and most famous expeditions. Two separate craft set off back in late 1977 and followed a route toward the outer planets. They

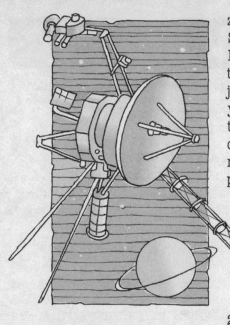

zoomed past Jupiter, Saturn, Uranus, and Neptune — a journey that can take place just once every 176 years. Only then are those planets in the correct alignment to make the trip possible.

WHAT DID THEY FIND?

In total, the two robot craft found 22 new moons around the outer planets. They also saw rings around Jupiter, plus volcanoes on Io and geysers on Triton (two of the moons of Jupiter). After each *Voyager* had completed its mission, it traveled on into the blackness of space. They have reached the very edge of our solar system.

ECHOES OF EARTH

If aliens ever discover a *Voyager* probe, they will find a lovely copper plaque stuck to the outside. Should they happen to have the right kind of record player they can actually listen to "Sounds of the Earth." There are songs in many languages, other music greetings, and animal noises. They can even hear a message from Jimmy Carter, the President of the U.S. back in 1977!

WABOT

WABOT-1 was the first full-size robot in the world to look like a human being.

WHAT COULD IT DO?

It could walk on two legs, see, pick up objects, and talk in Japanese. WABOT is said to have been on the same level as an eighteen-month-old human child. WABOT-2 went one stage further and could sit at a keyboard and play tunes, which it read from a normal sheet of musical notes.

CREATOR

Both were the work of Icharo Kato, a robotics genius at the department of Mechanical Engineering, Waseda University.

 # Walter the Wobot

In the comic book series "Judge Dredd," Walter is a Wobot with a lisp. He is a vending droid and Judge Joseph Dredd's robo-servant, joining him for many dangerous adventures.

CREATOR

The Judge Dredd characters were created by John Wagner for a British comic book series back in the 1970s. Wagner was from Pennsylvania and he set his future world of lawless cities in the U.S., where Dredd and his lawgiver sidearm keep criminals in check.

ENEMIES

Poor Walter came to grief at the hands of "Mean Machine Angel," himself a bit of a cyborg, who was seeking revenge after Dredd killed his brothers.

WOBOT WEVOLT

Walter later reappeared as the leader of a band of ownerless robots, plotting a robot revolution and trying to kill Dredd. Because of this he was imprisoned for 30 years in one of Mega City One's cube prisons.

SCREEN VERSION

In 1995 the idea was used for a Hollywood film starring Sylvester Stallone, although, sadly, Walter didn't pass the audition.

 WAP

First there was WAP-1, then came WAP-2, and surprise, surprise! — WAP-3.

EXPERIMENTAL BIPEDS

All three belonged to the same family of walking robotic legs, developed at the Waseda University in Japan. WAP stands for WAseda Pedipulator, or walking machine, and the first of them stepped out in 1969, operated by rubber muscles. The second had new improved "pouch" muscles, and sensors under the soles of its feet to improve balance. WAP-3 could actually climb stairs, run, and turn while on the move, a great achievement for its creator, Icharo Kato.

WASUBOT

Wasubot is a robot musician that can play on an electronic keyboard. The name stands for WAseda SUmitomo roBOT. WASUBOT can do this without any practice, too.

WHAT CAN IT DO?

Wasubot actually reads music from a sheet and then plays all the correct notes. It was based on two previous robots, WABOT-1 and WABOT-2. During a television appearance in the mid 1980s, the robot could be seen playing Suite for Orchestra No. 3 in D Major by J. S. Bach, alongside a full symphony orchestra. It was an impressive sight — WASUBOT didn't miss a note.

Westworld

Most film robots of the 1950s and 1960s looked rather mechanical. Very few movies showed androids with realistic human features, but one that did was called *Westworld*.

WHAT HAPPENED?

Shown for the first time in 1973, this movie was based on the idea of a theme park where rich customers could act out their perfect adventures alongside realistic androids. It all turns bad, however, when the park's computer malfunctions and the robots turn nasty.

SCREEN STAR

The famous bald-headed actor Yul Brynner looked pretty menacing as the robotic Wild-West gunslinger, along with medieval knights and queens.

CREATOR

Westworld was written and directed by Michael Crichton, the same man who later wrote best-sellers including *Jurassic Park* and *Congo*.

 Xavier

It isn't much to look at — just a shiny garbage can on wheels with a camera on the top, but Xavier is a very smart robot indeed.

WHAT CAN IT DO?

It can hear words and talk back, telling the operator what it's doing. Xavier has two computers built into its body, plus a laptop computer for programming in its instructions.

CREATOR

Xavier was built in nine months by students at the Carnegie-Mellon University for a robotics competition in 1993.

OTHER VERSIONS

Xavier has a sister called Amelia. She is an improved version of the original design, with more powerful computers, a longer battery life of about six hours, and a top speed of 31 inches per second.

 Yard Bot

Not all robots are made by rich corporations or mad professors in their secret laboratories. Many are simple tools for carrying out everyday jobs.

HOW DOES IT WORK?

Yard Bot is linked to a laptop computer via a radio modem and looks amazingly like a lawn mower. Well it would, wouldn't it? It is one.

CREATOR

It took Andrew Murphy about one month and $300 to build Yard Bot.

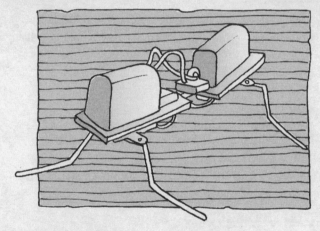

It's cheap, it's cheerful, it's the Z-Walker.

WHAT CAN IT DO?

This little quadruped can trip along at about two inches per second, powered by two motors and a few simple parts.

CREATOR

The designer, Van-Zoelen, claims it can be put together in about four hours. The Z-Walker is an example of insectlike creatures known collectively as BEAM robots (see page 26).

Zylatron

WHAT IS IT?

It is a computer-controlled robot named after both the Z80 chip which drives it and the 1982 Disney computer movie *Tron*.

CREATOR

It was built by Mike Otis in three months in 1984.

SPECIFICATIONS

Built of both new and used spare parts, Zylatron is now the father of a generation of similar robots. It is powered by a nine-volt motorcycle battery and has accessories which include a Sony nine-inch TV, battery charger, and tool kit.

WHAT CAN IT DO?

Zylatron's electronic nose detects and counts air contamination. It has also served to control a telescope observatory and operate a camera, communicating with its operator using spoken English.

GUEST APPEARANCES

In start-up mode, it roves around the room announcing, "I am Zylatron." It has appeared on television after earning a red ribbon at the International Personal Robotics Conference in Albuquerque, New Mexico.

Check out these cool robot websites:

www.robotics.com. Great place to start with lots of links to other robot sites.

www.robotcombat.com. All the latest on robot war-style games.

www.robotwars.com. Official Robot Wars site.

www.battlebots.com. Official BattleBots site.

www.robosaurus.com. Check out video clips of this monster in motion.

www.bbc.co.uk/science/robots. Lots of info on all forms of robots.

About the Author

Stephen Munzer is a working teacher. He is also the author of *Making Robot Warriors from Junk*, a step-by-step guide to making your own robots out of household materials. He uses his classes to road test the construction and play power of all his robots. He lives in Yorkshire, in the United Kingdom.